The McMullan Family in New Zealand

2nd Edition

The 20th century story of Thomas McMullan and Beatrice Howe-Johns and their family

Randall McMullan

Published by Piano Beach

Auckland, New Zealand

www.pianobeach.com

ISBN 978-0-473-46309-0 Softcover format

ISBN 978-0-473-46310-6 PDF format

Cover photo: Thomas McMullan and Beatrice Howe-Johns. Probably a portrait for their marriage in 1899.

Contents

Introduction

This collection of stories, facts and photos is about a family living in Otago, New Zealand in the first half of the twentieth century. The earlier family members had sailed across the world to live in New Zealand in the 1800s. They landed at South Island ports and found their ways to Central Otago where, following the Gold Rushes of the 1860s, the extraction of gold continued to support communities. Indeed, our branch of the family not only lived in the junction town of Lawrence but had their home in Gabriels Gully where the Gold Rush of the 1860s began.

The information centres on Thomas McMullan and Beatrice Howe-Johns, and their 8 children. Between them they lived from the 1870s until the 2000s. As with most families, their lives were both ordinary and special. Their ordinary lives helped to build a country and their special lives formed us who are descended from them. Rather than find gold they made it – gold of the family type.

Looking at the wider picture, there are 4 migrant family streams that made up the McMullan family in New Zealand. They are –

- **the *McMullin* family** from County Antrim, in the north of Ireland
- **the *Thompson* family** from Castledawson, County Derry/Londonderry in the north of Ireland
- **the *Johns* family** from Bickington, Devon, England
- **the *Kelly* family** from County Clare in the west of Ireland

Eight children from 100 years ago generate many descendants! I have concentrated on recording what we know about Thomas McMullan (mother's family name Thompson) and Beatrice Howe-Johns (mother's family name Kelly) and their family - as they are backbone of the family in the early twentieth century. As Nana and Granddad they were very real people to some of us. But time passes by and so do our memories pass unless we record them.

This book doesn't attempt to give information about the descendants of the 8 children of Thomas and Beatrice, or even describe their loving spouses. It does attempt to capture the personal stories and character echoes that do remain of the early McMullan children. All the branches of the later families are rich with information that deserves to be separately recorded.

The information is organised into chapters around family origins, family people and family places. Some of the information tends to be repeated, but this is probably no bad thing as there is a lot of information to take in. One strand of the family story is how the spelling of family names can vary, for a variety of reasons. The book takes its title from the spellings used by Thomas and Beatrice.

Thank you to everyone who supplied information, and special thanks to Gabrielle Dunne and Margaret McTear who gathered information and wrote it down so eloquently. The 'snippets' in their emails form much of the text of the book.

Randall McMullan May 2014

Introduction to the second edition

Sharing knowledge online brings new details. In this case, it is significant new knowledge about the Thompson family in Ireland and their migration to New Zealand. For some family members this was by way of the goldfields of Victoria, not a single voyage of the *Warrior Queen* to Dunedin as I assumed. By the time of that particular journey in 1866 journey two of the Thompson sisters were already married and living at Wetherstons, Lawrence. Their newly-widowed mother also came to Wetherstons with the remainder of the family.

I have left the format of the first edition intact, apart from a few inline revisions, and added a new section of *Later information* which focuses on the Thompson family in Ireland, Australia and New Zealand.

Randall McMullan November 2018

About the family information

It is now very much easier to get and to share family information via the internet. Much of the information about our early family now comes from other people's research, and from their family trees published online.

I have concentrated on establishing facts for people in New Zealand using birth, death and marriage certificates. This dry formal information does sometimes contain little surprises and mysteries; and that is just within New Zealand. The New Zealand unknowns of the last 150 years are a reminder that it is even harder to be certain about family happenings in England and Ireland many generations ago.

The first draft of this text used words like 'probably' and 'possibly'. They have now been minimised to make a better read. But it is worth keeping an open mind about all 'family facts' especially when we do not have direct knowledge.

For spelling the family names I have standardised on *McMullan* and *Howe-Johns* as these are the forms used by Thomas and Beatrice. But you will see in these pages that the family names appear and evolve in a variety of ways. Some of these variations are the result of official recorders or newspapers using different spellings. But some of the changes and evolutions in names were purposeful. A new life in a new place was perhaps a time for new name.

The photos are from many people and I have tended to use the older photos, to try and include all the McMullan children and spouses at some stage, and to choose some photos that are striking or interesting..

Above: **Thomas McMullan**, born in 1871, photographed in a Lawrence studio aged about 1 year. The studio dog is a prop.

Between family members we have many more photos and I suggest that future projects should include scanning photos and identifying them carefully. We can then keep them in electronic format, distribute them and share them via social websites.

The information shown in the family trees on the following pages is generated from a standard genealogy or 'family tree' computer program. I am happy to distribute the electronic contents to anyone interested so that it may live on and be improved.

Acknowledgements

Sources of illustration are from McMullan family members except for those listed below.

Gabriels Gully p3, Dunedin photo p5 – Hocken Library, University of Otago; Dunedin painting p5 – National Library of New Zealand; Clyde photo p7 – Te Papa Museum of New Zealand; Lawrence photo p27 – New Zealand Electronic Text Collection; Bickington photos pp 37,38 – Google Streetview; Thompson property p43 – Google Maps; Wetherstones photos p44 – Research Repository, University of Canterbury.

Ancestors of Thomas McMullan

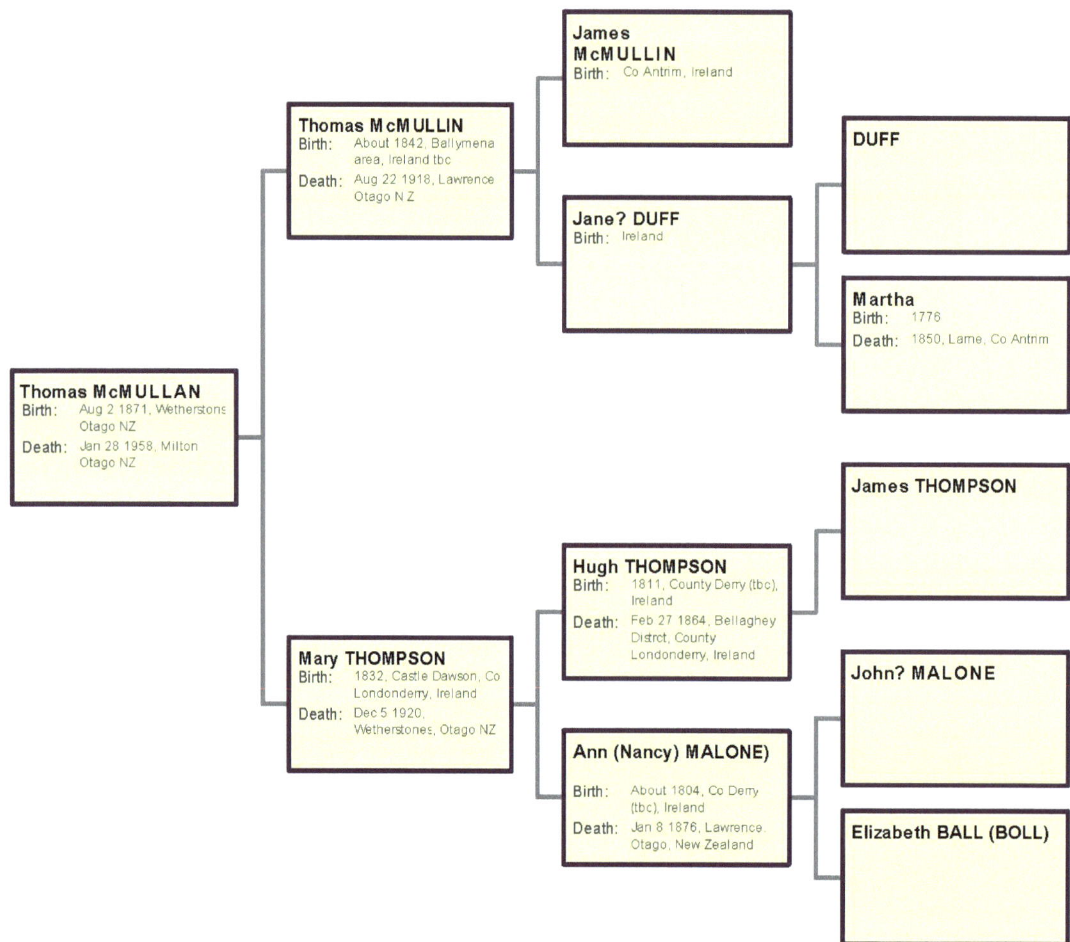

Ancestors of Beatrice Howe-Johns

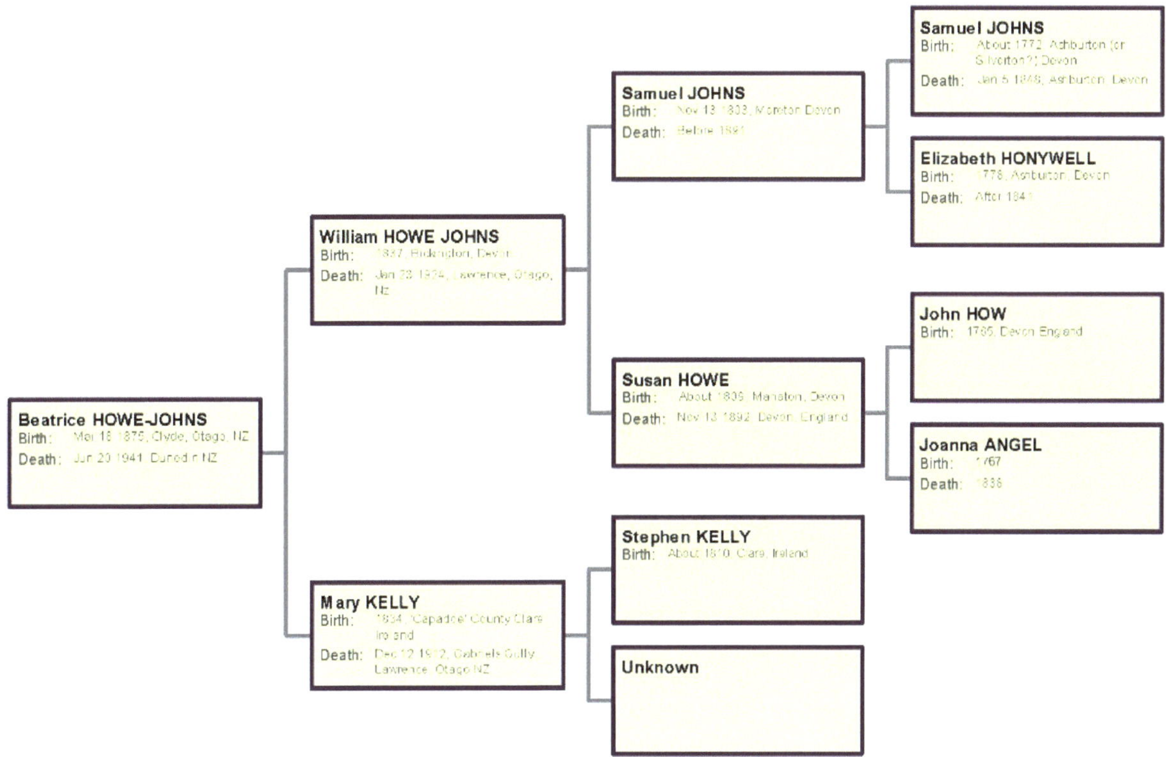

The Children of Thomas and Beatrice McMullan

The table below gives an overview of the lives of the McMullan Family children

Mary Marion Ellen "Molly" MCMULLAN		
Birth	23 Apr 1902	At home, Gabriels Gully Lawrence Otago
Death	12 May 1983	St Joseph's Rest Home, Brockville, Dunedin
Burial	14 May 1983	Andersons Bay Cemetery, Dunedin, Otago
Beatrice Iris "Babe" MCMULLAN		
Birth	10 Aug 1903	At home, Gabriels Gully, Lawrence, Otago
Death	24 Jan 1975	Oamaru Cemetery
Burial	Jan 1975	Oamaru Cemetery
Spouse	John Vincent ROONEY (1897–1974)	
Marriage	5 Aug 1930	Sacred Heart Church, North East Valley, Dunedin
Thomas William James "Jim" MCMULLAN		
Birth	25 May 1908	At home, Gabriels Gully Lawrence, Otago
Death	18 Jan 1976	Dunedin
Burial	18 Jan 1976	Andersons Bay Cemetery, Dunedin Otago
Spouse	Agnes Ross MCCALLION (1910-1996)	
Marriage	2 May 1928	St Joseph's Cathedral, Dunedin, Otago
Lawrence Gerard "Larry" MCMULLAN		
Birth	8 Sep 1911	Gabriels Gully Lawrence Otago
Burial	Jun 1977	Memorial Plaque at Napier Wharerangi Cemetery, Napier
Death	25 Jun 1977	Napier Hospital, Napier
Spouse	Agnes Adelaide RANDALL (1915-2002)	
Marriage	1939	Sacred Heart Basilica, Wellington
Jessie Margaret MCMULLAN		
Birth	23 Apr 1914	At home, Gabriels Gully Lawrence, Otago
Death	20 Dec 1978	Dunedin
Burial	23 Dec 1978	Andersons Bay Cemetery, Dunedin, Otago
Spouse	Francis Thomas HALL (1906-1975)	
Marriage	14 Apr 1940	St Joseph's Cathedral, Dunedin, Otago
Anne Therese "Nancy" MCMULLAN		
Birth	19 Sep 1915	At home, Gabriels Gully Lawrence Otago
Death	15 Jul 1990	Dunedin
Burial	15 Jul 1990	Green Park Cemetery, Dunedin, Otago
Spouse	John William MCCALLION (1910-1956)	
Kathleen Alannah MCMULLAN		
Birth	*19 Apr 1917*	*At home, Gabriels Gully Lawrence Otago*
Death	18 Nov 1989	Mosgiel, Otago, NZ
Burial	21 Nov 1989	East Taieri Cemetery, Mosgiel, Otago
Spouse	Ronald Walter COX (1916–1998)	
Marriage	1939	St Joseph's Cathedral, Dunedin, Otago
Dorothy MCMULLAN		
Birth	21 Jan 1920	Family Home, Gabriels Gully Lawrence Otago
Death	May 2003	Ranui Rest Home, Alexandra Otago
Burial	May 2003	Alexandra Cemetery, Alexandra, Otago
Spouse	Alexander William Henry WILSON (1916-2001)	
Marriage	4 Aug 1942	St Joseph's Cathedral, Dunedin, Otago

McMullan Family Origins

Church Island on Lough Beg nr Bellarghy, Co Derry, Ireland

Irish origins

In 1865, on a spring day in the North of Ireland, Mary Thompson aged 33 married Thomas McMullin aged 23. The wedding was in the village of Bellarghy which is half way between Belfast and Derry/Londonderry and close to the large inland water of Lough Neagh.

Family stories relate that Mary was staunch in her Church of Ireland (Anglican) beliefs, that Thomas visited on Sunday afternoons, but there were also other men courting her. Mary apparently had several dresses ready for marriage, so the Thompsons were perhaps a family with some money.

Thomas is recorded as being the son of *James McMullin* and family memories have the family origins as being a farm in the Ballymena area of Antrim, which is about 20 km from the Bellarghy area where Mary lived. By their name, the McMullin family would have been Presbyterian settlers who moved from Scotland to the Ulster 'Plantations' in the 1600s.

Thomas and Mary initially lived somewhere near the village of Bellaghy which lies between the Magherafelt and Ballymena, a few kilometres away from Castledawson where Mary was born. The first child of Thomas and Mary was born in Bellaghy on 1 April 1866 and recorded as Hugh McMullin.

Record of the Marriage
Marriage date: 13 May 1865
Place: St Tida's Church at Bellarghy, Parish of Ballyscullion, Londonderry, Ireland
Groom: Thomas McMullin, father James McMullin
Bride: Mary Thompson, father Hugh Thompson

Spelling Variations

The spelling of family names often depended on the recording person, such as the clergyman or the registrar of births, deaths and marriages.

In Ireland, Thomas's name was recorded as *McMullin* for his wedding to Mary. As it was for the birth of his son Hugh McMullin.

In New Zealand the births of his children were recorded as *McMullen* although later they mostly used the name *McMullan.*

Thomas and Mary appear in the electoral rolls of 1893, 1896 and 1911 with both their names always spelled *McMullin.* So we can perhaps assume that was an older spelling of the family name.

The McMullin family of three sailed for New Zealand in October 1866. They were accompanied by Mary's mother Ann, brother Jim Thompson and her sister Margaret.

Their ship was the *Warrior Queen* which made regular voyages between London Docks and Port Chalmers, Dunedin. The sailings were advertised in newspapers with the name of a local agent for the shipping line.

The Thompson-McMullin family perhaps had enough means to travel in greater comfort than sponsored migrants on other more crowded ships. However, all classes of passenger were subject to the same boisterous southern seas during the 99 days of this particular non-stop passage.

See the section on *Family Voyages* for more details of the McMullin family voyage and other family voyages to New Zealand in the sailing ships of the time.

Above: Map showing family areas in the Province of Ulster, Ireland. Also showing the relationship to Scotland where the earlier McMullin family originated

Life in New Zealand

Thomas, Mary and young Hugh arrived at Port Chalmers, Dunedin in early 1867 and probably went straight to the Wetherstons goldfields where two of Mary's sisters were established with families. Thomas is noted in electoral records of the 1870s as a 'miner' and around this date the gold industry was evolving from small workings to larger scale extraction of the metal by sluicing, dredging and crushing.

From the earliest birth registrations and electoral rolls the McMullan family home or small farm is recorded as being at *Wetherstones Flat* on the edge of Lawrence in an area now occupied by the Lawrence Golf Club. Family memories recall that the old family house was the first golf club house.

Mary and Thomas's first child born in New Zealand was Mary, recorded as being born in 1868 at Wetherstons with her father's occupation being a 'miner'. As Gabriels Gully and Wetherstons were worked for gold, the settlement at the mouth of the gully became the town of *Lawrence*, originally known as The Junction, Tuapeka. In 1877 the railway arrived in Lawrence as a branch line connected to the Main South Line near Milton. The railway ran alongside the family property at Wetherstons.

The family home of Thomas and Mary McMullan seems to have remained at Wetherstones Flat over the decades of the nineteenth century as the children grow up, marry and have children. We catch glimpses of the McMullan name in electoral lists, school rolls and newspaper reports children

Some of the reports are sad news of deaths. Hugh, the eldest child and born in Ireland, died in 1884 at the young age of 18 years. The death certificate gives the cause of death as peritonitis, after 7 days of illness. Young Hugh's occupation is recorded as 'farm labourer'.

Dates of Thomas and Mary McMullin's Children

Hugh	1866 – 1884
Mary	1868 –1962
James	1869 – 1944
Thomas	1871 –1958
John	1873 – tbc

Above: Painting of early mining in Gabriels Gully by John Turnbull Thompson

A second son, James, was born to Thomas and Mary in 1869. He appears in the School Admission Records in 1876 and is known to have married and had a daughter.

The third son is 'our' Thomas who started the family which is the focus of this book. Thomas McMullan was born on 2 August 1871, although when his family buried him in 1958 he was recorded as being several years younger than his real age!

Another son, John (Jack) was born in 1873 and, at this stage, we know nothing about him. Daughter Mary married a Samuel Bayliss and had two children, Ella and Bertram.

We don't know if Mary McMullin was very active in the life of the Anglican church in Lawrence. One of her sons, young Thomas, had married a Catholic wife Beatrice Howe-Johns and their children went to the church school of Saint Patricks in Lawrence. Their home, on the edge of Lawrence in Gabriels Gully was a short walk from their grandparent's house at Wetherstones.

Below: Wetherstones Flat – site of McMullan farm

Around 1891 Ella Bayliss had a love child, William, who was brought up at Wetherstones by his grandparents, Thomas and Mary. He was later known as Bill McMillan. Bill worked on the railways and married Ruby Rooney from Roxburgh. They later lived in Hastings and were 'Aunty Ruby and Uncle Bill' to young Randall McMullan who lived in Napier.

While Bill McMillan was away at World War One, his young wife Ruby lived with old Tom and Mary at Wetherstones. In later life she had a good memory of family members and their stories which she passed on.

Mary's brother and sisters, some of whom travelled with her from Ireland on the *Warrior Queen,* also lived in the Lawrence area. While at the Victoria gold rush before Wetherstones, Sarah married Samuel Anderson and Elizabth married John Pearson. See page 42 for more information.

Below: Early Lawrence, showing Anglican Church

Electoral rolls continued to list Thomas McMullin as a *miner* and possibly over the decades he continued to work with the various companies that continued sluicing and dredging for gold over several decades after the 1860s Gold Rush.

Ruby McMillan recalled that 'Old Tom never recovered from a broken leg' and this is verified on his 1918 death certificate; extracts shown nearby. His father's name is listed as James McMullan, farmer, and his mother as Annie McMullan, formerly Duffy.

Mary died a couple of years later in 1920 and her death certificate intriguingly records her maiden surname as Thompson, but her surname 'at birth' as being 'Malone'. The information on a death certificate is filled in by those left behind but perhaps someone, like Bill McMillan, did have that information.

The certificate also confirms that Mary was about 10 years older than Tom, and this difference is also recorded in the record of their marriage at Bellarghy, Ireland in 1865. Presumably theirs was a marriage of love that overcame some initial difficulties and one that came on a long journey.

Thomas McMullan - Death Certificate Extracts

Date: 22 August 1918 *Place:* Weatherstones
Cause: Facture of Femur, Traumatic fever and shock
Age: 76 Where born: Ireland *Years in NZ*: 55
Issue living: 3 sons, 1 daughter

Mary McMullan - Death Certificate Extracts

Date: 5 December 1920 *Place:* Weatherstones
Cause: Senile Decay, Cardiac failure - sudden
Age: 88 Where born: Castle Dawson North of Ireland
Years in NZ: 58
Issue living: 3 sons, 1 daughter

Spelling Variations

The variations in spelling of the family name continued in the Anglican Section of Lawrence Cemetery where Tom and Mary are buried. Although their death certificates record 'McMullan', their gravestone uses 'McMillan'.

Perhaps it was their grandson Bill McMillan who arranged the gravestone. Tom and Mary had used an *i* in their name – but as *McMullin*

Howe-Johns Family Origins

Above: **Dunedin about 1861** – A romantic image by W S Hatton

On a Dunedin summer's day of March 1863, Mary Kelly aged 29 from County Clare Ireland married William Johns aged 26 from Devon England. The couple were married by the French priest Father Moreau, in his house, at Duncan Street.

We have to speculate about the early lives of Mary and William, helped along by some bare information from official records, by histories of those times and places, plus a few family memories.

We do have more information about their later lives but, for the moment, no photos of them. We have a small image of William's father Samuel. Perhaps the photo, on a later page, of their daughter Beatrice, taken around 1899, contains something of the likenesses of both Mary and William.

In electoral lists of the 1870s William states that he is a miner so perhaps he had been to the goldfields and was back in Dunedin when he met and married Mary. From her Irish name and origin we can assume that Mary was the Catholic while William, whose father was baptised in a non-conformist chapel, came from an English rural background with no strong religious convictions. And a stronger love for Mary.

Below: **Photo of Dunedin about 1861** – Showing the gritty realities

The marriage certificate for the couple lists the place of marriage as being 'The house of Rev D Moreau, Duncan Street'. Father Delphine Moreau was one of a number of priests from the French Marist order who served the needs of Otago before formal parishes were established. In 1862 he laid the foundation stone of the Dunedin's early St Joseph's church.

The first Catholic church in Dunedin was blessed by Bishop Viard in 1864. The brick church still exists, as part of St Joseph's School, near the present St Joseph's Cathedral

William's background

Family stories from the days of William's old age says that he 'jumped ship' to go to the goldfields. One variation is that it was from a whaling ship in Australia. In NZ electoral lists of the 1870s William states that he is a 'miner'. Many early New Zealanders were British merchant seaman who didn't return to their ships for the return voyage. If caught, the sailors lost any wages due and had to serve about 12 weeks in prison; about half the Dunedin prisoners recorded between 1850 and 1860 were sailors. We have no record of William ever being caught but if he was listed somewhere then that was perhaps a reason why he gradually changed his name during his life in New Zealand.

William arrived in NZ as *William Johns,* became *William How Johns* filed under the letter J, and he ended as *William Howe-Johns* filed under the letter H.

Above: Great Staple Tor on Dartmoor, Devon

William was born in 1837 in the county of Devon, England to mother Susan (born Hows) and father Samuel Johns. We have reasonably accurate information about William's family – thanks to public records in England which started in 1837 and to the research of other people with Johns family descendants. William is recorded as the second eldest of at least 8 children mainly born in and around the village of Bickington, Devon.

Bickington and its region is a strip of South Devon between the high ground of Dartmoor and the sea shore at Teignmouth. The area is within 10 kilometres of Newton Abbot and within 10 kilometres of the pretty old town of Ashburton. Today, the nearby Devon Expressway speeds traffic further down the peninsular to Plymouth and Cornwall. But most of the local roads are actually the popular vision of quiet, lush and narrow English country lanes with the tall hedges trying to meet overhead. A few kilometres to the West the land rises to Dartmoor where trees cease and the barren landscape features rocky outcrops called *tors* and the remains of stone age settlements. William would meet a similar stark landscape in Central Otago.

William's father Samuel and mother Susan Howes were married at nearby Manaton, Devon in 1831. William's father, Samuel Johns born in 1803, was the son of another Samuel born in 1772 who married an Elizabeth Honywell. Other earlier family names include North or Northcott, and Angel. The names of the sisters of 'our' William included Susan, Mary and Emily which were also used for his children in New Zealand. This is probably more than coincidence, particularly for a man who changed his name to include his mother's surname of How.

Right: **Samuel Johns** born 1803. William's father

In the 1851 census a William Johns, aged 13 born in Bickington, is recorded as living as a farm labourer in the extended household of farmer Thomas Mann at Gale near Bickington. The Gale farm contained 7 family members and 3 employees. The same census records William's father, Samuel Johns, living in Bickington nearby with his wife and 4 children younger than William.

It was a period when farming was in decline along with the Devon's industries connected with wool and cloth making. But railways were bringing the new industry of tourism, especially to the coastal towns.

Mary's background

We don't yet know much about Mary before her arrival in Lyttleton Harbour, Canterbury on 6th May 1861 aboard the 881 ton ship *Rhea Sylvia.* The voyage from Bristol had taken 111 days and had started as a very rough one for the 152 passengers when off the English coast the ship met a succession of gales that lasted a fortnight. On the night of January 27 a tremendous sea broke over the ship, water got below, the binnacle was washed overboard, the gig stove in, and all livestock was lost. The *Lyttleton Times* of 8 May 1861 reports that the relieved passengers signed a testimonial to Captain Charles Evans.

Above: Mary Kelly entry in record book of the *Assisted Emigration to Canterbury, New Zealand by the Ship Rh Sylvia*

The NZ government emigration records for the ship total 19 single women and list Mary as a 21 year old Farm Servant from Galway. Like most of the single women she signed a promissory note to the Canterbury Provincial Government for 7 pounds of the 11 pounds cost of the voyage. Single women willing to work were valuable to New Zealand, and of course valuable to the many single men in the Colony who needed wives.

Shipping records were not always accurate about ages and Mary seems to have been older than 21 in 1861 when she arrived in New Zealand. Mary's NZ death certificate of 1912 records her birth place as being in Capadoe, County Clare, Ireland, which is the county just south of the major centre of Galway. 'Capadoe' does not seem to exist as a place and may be a mis-pronounced or mis-remembered name entered by the person completing the death certificate. Cratloe is a real village in County Clare. Apart from the name of Stephen Kelly as Mary's father we do not yet know more about the family

See the section on *Migrant Ships* for more details of the McMullan family voyage and other family voyages to New Zealand in the sailing ships of the time.

Married Life

After their wedding in 1863 Mary and William probably returned to a Central Otago area of gold mining – William's stated occupation was that of 'miner'. After the first discovery of gold at Gabriels Gully in 1861 the goldfields had spread around Central Otago and included areas near Cromwell, Queenstown, and Naseby. In 1868 we know the couple lived in the Clyde area so perhaps that was an initial destination.

Above: **Clyde in 1870s** – Photo by Burton Bros

James was Willam and Mary's first child and, although he is not been found in the Birth register system, he was probably born in 1863 relatively soon after their marriage. This would agree with Mary's death certificate of 1912 which lists an eldest son aged about 50.

The first child found recorded in official records is **Susan,** born in 1 August 1868 in Clyde. William's occupation is recorded as 'Gold Miner' and his residence being at 'Jacks Clyde'. Meanwhile another daughter, **Mary**, was born before Susan in about 1865. Mary's death notice in 1937 describes her as 'eldest daughter' and she is buried with her parents in Lawrence cemetery.

Other known children include: Anne who married a Gerard O'Connor; William ('Billy") who went to school at Albert Town and became blacksmith at Becks and had a garage at Clyde; Beatrice, who later married Thomas McMullan, was born in 1875 and was the first child to have the birth registered under 'How Johns' instead of 'Johns'. There was possibly a younger daughter Emily.

In the 1870s the (How) Johns family lived in the town of Clyde (also known then as Upper Dunstan). William appears in the regular electoral rolls under surname Johns, with first names of William How. The electoral rolls don't record William's occupation at this time but the gold industry continued with the larger scale work using stamper batteries and river dredges.

Clyde was also the site of a major crossing of the Clutha river using a punt ferry. Crossing the rivers of New Zealand was a necessary and dangerous activity and the Clutha is New Zealand's swiftest and highest volume river. At the Clyde crossing a bridge was completed in 1876 but was washed away in 1878. The punt service started again in March 1879 'with William Howjohns as the puntman.' The Clyde punt was finally replaced by a new bridge in 1881.

By 1884 William's electoral address is Luggate and his occupation is listed as puntman. Luggate, near current Wanaka airport, is further up the Clutha River from Clyde and was a river crossing on the main route from Cromwell to the Lake Hawea area. The Luggate ferry punt opened in 1882 and we might assume that William was the first puntman and possibly had a house down on the river bank so as to be on call for travellers. It was not always a quiet life as the nearby 1888 newspaper accounts show.

The local Vincent Council also opened a punt ferry across the Clutha at Albert Town, 10km up the river from Luggate and close to

Birthdates of William and Mary's Children:

James abt 1863	Mary abt 1865
William 1873	Susan 1868
	Anne 1871
	Beatrice 1875
	Emily tbc

Above: **Clyde Bridge** – About 1900

Punts were flat floating platforms connected to the other side of the river by a steel cable. When the punt was steered correctly the current of the river pushed the punt across the river. There were very few bridges across rivers and early bridges were destroyed by floods. Travellers and communities depended heavily upon the punts for many things, from receiving essential goods to attending school or church. There were many vigorous 'discussions' about the costs of a punt crossing and sometimes complaints about the puntman, especially when he didn't answer a call from the other side of the river.

Above: **The Luggate Punt** – showing platform loaded with waggon and horses

Wanaka township (then known as Pembroke). Council and newspaper records show that William also worked on the Albert Town punt.

What's in a name?

Starting with Susan in 1868 family births are recorded under the surname *Johns*, with both parents having a second name of *How*. This continued until 1875 when Beatrice is recorded under a surname of *How Johns*

Meanwhile we can assume that Mary Johns was kept very busy with keeping house. She would have been helped by Susan who never married and was later a teacher. Another daughter, perhaps Emily, is recorded as dying early.

We get happier impressions from newspaper reports of family weddings in 1899 and 1906 which praised the 'capital cooking' of Mrs Howejohns. Daughter Mary is also mentioned in the Otago Witness newspaper under 'Ladies Matters' as attending a couple of balls and functions in Wanaka and Hawea. At the Oddfellow Ingleside at Cromwell in 1893 Miss Howejohns was wearing a 'pretty dress of cream, with blue chiffon'

Beatrice, the Howe Johns daughter, from whom many of us are descended was married to Thomas McMullan in Albert Town 1899. The newspaper account tells us that the school was closed, that there was creature comforts in abundance, and that dancing 'was kept up all night!' The couple then left to live in Lawrence.

At the time of Annie's wedding in 1906 William was almost 70 years old and Mary was 72. At some stage after 1906 they moved to Lawrence where daughter Beatrice lived with husband Tom McMullan. In 1909 the Water Works committee of the Borough council received a report from William Howjohns the 'Race Caretaker' about repairing 'leaks under the boxes' of the water supply and about someone tampering with the 'water gate at the big dam'. William had a son also called William, but 'Billy' was a blacksmith at Becks so presumably the Race Caretaker was William himself – still involved in 'things watery'.

From *The Tuapeka Times*, 29 December 1888:

On Wednesday morning about ten o'clock the Luggate punt, near Cromwell, on which was the Luggate mill waggon, and a team of four horses, was carried away while crossing the Clutha river. It appears that the upper punt collapsed, and getting waterlogged sank so deeply into the water that the leading rope broke. The whole was then swept down the river as far as the Devil's Whirlpool, where the men and horses (the latter had been loosed meanwhile) swam ashore. The punts and the waggon were completely wrecked. Fortunately the waggon contained only about 1000 ft sawn timber and a few bags of flour. The accident is not due to any carelessness on the part of the puntkeeper.

Above: Sarah and William How-Johns (brother of our Beatrice), around 1905

Another Howe Johns wedding, for daughter Annie, took place in 1906 at Hawea,

The Otago Witness reports:

After the ceremony was over the party came back to Albertown and partook of the wedding breakfast. Many happy little speeches were made, and. Mrs Howejohns was praised for the excellent arrangements and her capital cookery, and everyone looked uncommonly pleased and happy. The farming visitors then mostly went home, as this is the time of the year when the stock requires a lot of attention

Mary died in Lawrence on the 12 December 1912 and her death certificate records the cause as 'cardiac degeneration and valvular incompetence - for 3 years'. The Otago Daily times listed the death as *Howe-Johns, Mary wife of William (d 12 Dec 1912, aged 78 years) at her residence Lawrence.* Mary was buried in Lawrence cemetery on 14 December 1912. William was buried with Mary in January 1924 after dying of 'cerebral apoplexy' (stroke) at the age of 86.

Both death certificates are registered under the surname of 'Howe-Johns' so the change of name from Johns was complete at the end. Both certificates record their 'living issue' as being 2 sons and 5 daughters.

William's death certificate also records the maiden name of his mother Susan as being 'Martin' instead of How.

The England census of 1891 has Susan How living as mother in law to a Charles and Emma Martin, hence the name confusion perhaps. Knowledge of the Martin name seems to indicate that there was some contact across the oceans between William and the mother for whom he had so determinedly changed his name.

Above: **Howe-Johns Grave** – Lawrence Cemetery 2011

One of the Howe-Johns daughters, Susan, remained unmarried and became a teacher of Home Economics. She travelled around the Domincan Colleges at Invercargill, Dunedin and Teschemakers at Oamaru.

Later Susie lived with her sister Annie at Cosy Dell cottage in Gabriels Gully, looking after their father William until he died in 1924. The sisters moved to South Dunedin where they were favourite aunts of the McMullan children.

From St Patrick's College, Teschemakers magazine, 1914-1918:

Miss Howjohns came once a week to give us cooking lessons. No particular uniform was required for this, just well scrubbed hands and a white apron.

How well I remember those cooking lessons in the Convent kitchen, the large white kitchen table down the centre, and a monstrous black range with a double oven – it simply devoured the coal. The scones and buns we made graced the table for tea on Friday nights.

Compliments and criticisms flew at that meal. But who cared, we achieved something!

Molly Heffernan

The McMullan Family People

This chapter is about 'our' family branch of McMullans and Howe-Johns. Thomas, son of Thomas and Mary McMullan married Beatrice daughter of William and Mary Howe-Johns on Wednesday on 3 October 1899. Thomas was aged 28 and Beatrice was 24. The wedding was reported in the *Otago Witness* (see nearby box) as being held at the Howejohns' house and gives a glimpse of Beatrice as being 'a great favourite' with the residents of Albertown (Albert Town). There was 'creature comfort provided in abundance' and there was dancing all night!

Beatrice and Thomas were to have a family of eight children. The eldest child, Mary Marion known as Molly, was born in 1902 and lived until 1983. The youngest child, Dorothy, was born in 1920 and lived until 2003. Many of us knew both Molly and Dorothy, together with the other six children born in between. The family spanned the twentieth century – they were our mothers and fathers, grandmothers and grandfathers – and more.

From the *Otago Witness*, Issue 2380, 12 October 1899, Page 28

Albertown

Wedding - A wedding was solemnised in the township last Wednesday week, Mr Thomas McMillan, of Lawrence, being married at the house of the bride's father to Miss Beatrice Howejohns, the youngest daughter of Mr William Howejohns, the puntman. The Rev. Father Hunt, from Cromwell, performed the ceremony. Father Hunt is a favourite wherever he goes. As Mr Howejohns was a member of the school committee and sometimes chairman, and Miss Beatrice was formerly one of its scholars, the school was closed for half a day. The residents all turned out to celebrate the happy event, the bride being a great favourite. The ceremony over, those present partook of the good things and creature comforts provided in abundance, after which there were dancing and games on the green to the strains of Mr Harry Mackay's pipes. When darkness set in dancing began in good earnest, and was kept up all night, everyone voting the affair a most decided success, and many times over wishing the happy couple health, wealth, and prosperity. A few days afterwards they left for their new home, near Lawrence.

Beatrice and Thomas McMullan

Meanwhile we can sense and see the lives of the parents Thomas and Beatrice unfolding through all their children, through the events in their lives, the places they lived in, and in the photos that remain with us. We also have official documents such as records of births, deaths and marriages that. These records seem sterile at first but they reveal facts, such as unexpected deaths, that would have caused great sadness. Plus the records can hint at 'attitudes' to life such as how names were spelled, how they described themselves.

Left: **Tom McMullan** as baby

Remarkably, we do have a photo of baby Tom taken when he was about a year old. In order to make the long exposure needed by cameras of the time, the studio in Lawrence has young Tom gripped in a costume that is probably not his. Alongside him sits a dog so motionless that it must be a stuffed studio prop.

Young Tom had grown up living at the Wetherstones farm of his parents Tom and Mary McMullan. The records of the Wetherstones school, near his home, list him leaving school in 1887 with his destination recorded as being to 'work at home'. He was then aged 16 which was old for a school leaver of that time.

Tom's granddaughter Beatrice (McDermott) recalls him as being a very bright man who wanted to go teaching but was prevented by an injury that had made him blind in one eye.

When Tom McMullan died in 1958, his children thought that he was a couple of years younger than the near 87 years he really was. By his birth certificate he was born at *Wetherstones*, Lawrence in August 1871

A memory of Beatrice McDermott about her Grandfather Thomas:

He was quite fluent in the Maori language and able to quote long screeds of poetry, even in his later years

Below: **Early McMullan Children** – Babe, Molly, Jim – 1908

Above: **Babe holding baby Jessie, with Lawrence** – in front of the McMullan Cottage around 1915

Children born to Thomas and Beatrice McMullan	
William Harold Thomas	1901
Mary Marion Ellen (Molly)	1902
Beatrice Iris (Babe)	1903
Thomas William James (Jim)	1908
Lawrence Gerard (Larry)	1911
Jessie Margaret	1914
Annie Teresa (Nancy)	1915
Kathleen Alannah	1917
Dorothy	1920

Beatrice Howe-Johns was the daughter of William and Mary and grew up as one of the youngest in a family of 4 sisters and 2 brothers. Beatrice was born in Clyde and as a teenager she grew up in Luggate and Albert Town where her father was the Puntman. Wanaka (called Pembroke), Hawea and Cromwell were the larger nearby settlements where social life occurred.

Beatrice was gifted in needlework, handwork and knitting. Although a busy mother she was noted as being smartly dressed and for keeping the family very well-dressed. She received gifts of money from her father William Howe-Johns who lived nearby in Gabriels Gully until he died in 1924

.

The McMullan Children

Beatrice and Thomas actually had nine children but the first child, named William Harold Thomas, died about one month after his birth in 1901. In April 1902 Mary Marion, known as Molly, was born and the youngest child, Dorothy, was born in 1920. The children all thrived without serious incidents and enjoyed childhood in Lawrence and later in Dunedin.

The lives of family members were often intertwined but the following sections highlight some of the key events and memories associated with each child.

Mary Marion McMullan (Molly)

Molly was born at home in the cottage at Gabriels Gully, Lawrence and baptised at St Patrick's Church, Lawrence. As the eldest she was remembered as being very responsible and caring for the younger children. But, as a meticulous cleaner, she used to lock the younger siblings outside after she had cleaned the house!

As youngsters, Molly and her sister Babe (Beatrice) were sent on Saturdays to clean the home of their Howe-Johns Grandparents nearby in Gabriels Gully. Molly did the cleaning while Babe sat and chatted with their Grandma. Each week a half crown was given to Babe who knew she didn't earn it and happily handed it over to Molly, at their mother's request!

So thrilled were Molly and Babe when a girl was born after having two brothers, that they went into the village a brought home an elaborate dress for baby Jessie. Their mother sent them straight back to return it.

Molly studied music, gained qualifications in singing and then did nursing training in Dunedin from 1922 to 1926. In 1932 she entered the Brigidine Order of Religious Sisters in Masterton where she taught music at St Brides School. Recurring rheumatic fever caused Molly to leave the Order and for the next year she lived with William and Ruby McMillan in Hastings. In 1940, Molly finished her Post-Grad Nursing Diploma in Wellington.

Below: Molly as young nurse

Molly was a very well-qualified nurse and nursed all her life. She was Night Superintendent at Dunedin Public Hospital and, as Tutor Sister in Dunedin and Balclutha, she took some nieces under her wing while they did training. In 1950 Molly went to the Holy Year Celebrations in Rome, and did another trip to Europe in 1968 after her retirement.

Molly was noted as being a gatherer of goods and chattels and she passed them on to "more needing folk". As District Nurse in the Balclutha and Milton area 'Sister Molly' was well-placed to know folk in need and she was nominated for the MBE award for services to the community. Such was the community respect for Molly that, when she retired, they gave her a memorable send-off in the Milton Coronation Hall.

> Molly quoted iin local newspaper 1967::
>
> *My interests are gardening, singing and music. I am going to retire to my cottage at Chrystalls beach which has a nice little garden and I'll have time to settle in there before I leave for overseas next year. I want to go to Ireland because I have many friends there.*

Molly's family and friends also remember, sort of fondly, her habit of making them unscheduled visits, especially at meal times!

Molly lived a happy retirement life in Milton and at her cottage at Chrystalls Beach near Milton. Her final yearswere at the Kinmont home at Mosgiel, and then the Sacred Heart retirement home at Brockville in Dunedin run by the Little Sisters of the Poor.

When Molly died she was on her way to the Rosary in the little Sisters' Chapel. Her siblings were called and Kathleen was concerned because her sister was very warm! No wonder, as she was lying "in state" on her electric blanket - she obviously intended retiring early! On the following day, when Kathleen's family was removing Molly's possession, they found several silk stockings used as money boxes!

Below: **Babe and Molly** – Girls with hair

Beatrice Iris McMullan (Babe)

Babe (Beatrice) was born at home in Gabriels Gully cottage in August 1903 and baptised at St Patrick's Church, Lawrence. She is remembered as being a popular, musical, and sporty person who enjoyed all outdoor activities. At Gabriels Gully Babe made many a dash, when a younger sibling went missing, to check the potentially dangerous water race near the cottage. She was also very good sprinter at events. As a teen she represented her district in hockey.

At age 16 Babe was taken by ambulance from Lawrence to Dunedin Public Hospital with peritonitis and very nearly lost her life. She survived but always remembered the potholes and twisty road and, because of the red ambulance blankets, always refused to have any bed covers coloured red.

Babe was dux of St. Patrick's School, Lawrence, and to further her education she went to the Dominican College, *Teschemakers*, Oamaru. She travelled by train from Lawrence to the Teschemaker's Railway Siding, 8 miles south of Oamaru, where the boarders were met and had to walk the last few miles beside the horse and dray which carried their tin trunks.

Babe's first letter home from boarding school had to be rewritten because she asked after her dog, before asking after family members. Her young scamps of brothers, Jim and Lawrence, had threatened to skin her dog and hang it up!

Babe had a burst appendix at age 16 but survived well and walked the Milford Track at the age of 55 - quite a notable feat in those days.

Babe graduated as a registered nurse from the Oamaru Public Hospital. In Oamaru she met John Rooney who was mourning the death of his sister Kathleen, who died in child birth. The custom was for family members to wear a black band on the arm for a year and to refrain from socialising.

Babe was a good seamstress and embroiderer. She was known to take down her own curtains to make evening dresses for friends and younger siblings. (A similar 'repurposing' of curtains happens in *The Sound of Music*!)

Above:**1930 Wedding photo** showing Howard Rooney, Beatrice and John Rooney, Molly McMullan

Babe and John married after Babe graduated as a nurse. They bought a house adjacent to the family farm with the intention of moving into the Rooney Homestead. This didn't eventuate because Howard, John's brother, married a few years later and stayed on in the Homestead. So the house was kept, renovated often, and became the home which is still in the family today. It was here that all Babe's siblings and their children enjoyed an Open Home.

Babe was an Inaugural member of the Oamaru Catholic Women's League. In 1953 Babe and John went to the Eucharistic Congress in Sydney. Seasickness caused Babe to spent the four days on her bunk. To everyone's consternation, she opened the porthole to get fresh air and lay there while everyone cleaned up the water. Babe and John travelled around NZ in their caravan before retiring to Dunedin to 6 Bayfield Road, Anderson's Bay. Gardening and nursing at Chalet and St David Street Hospitals, then Eventide Home, kept her busy.

Thomas William James (Jim)

Jim was born at home in Gabriels Gully in May 1908 and baptised at St Patrick's Church, Lawrence. In early stories he is remembered as loving animals, being musical and being athletic.

We have a 1922 photo of Jim in his rugby team in Lawrence. Jim loved outdoor activities, especially riding and caring for horses at his McMullan grandparent's property at Wetherstones.

In a childhood prank remembered by family, Jim and his brother Larry hitched their sister Babe's dog to a cart. They then paraded along the main street of Lawrence calling out 'Pies for sale, pies for sale'.

Apparently Jim found the family move to Dunedin difficult. But, after a 5-year apprenticeship in Dunedin, he became a sought-after painter and decorator. But could doubtless done have been many other things in different times.

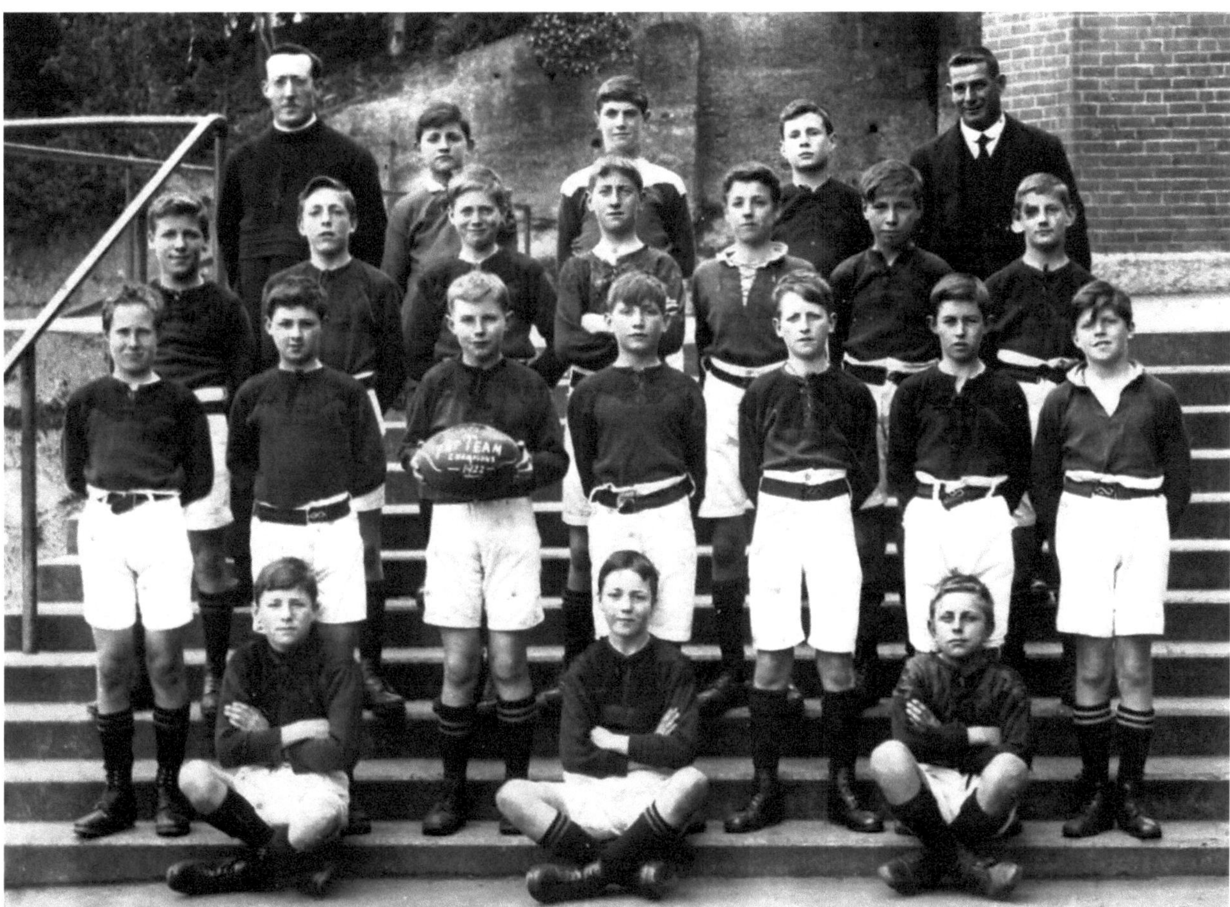

Above: **St Patrick's rugby team, Lawrence 1922** – Jim McMullan seated front left

Jim was a member of the NZ Territorial Army in the Otago Mounted Rifles and later he would serve again during World War II. Jim met Agnes McCallion at the 1925/26 International Exhibition which was held just behind the family home in Harbour Terrace. They were married at St Joseph's Cathedral Dunedin in May 1928.

In the 1930s Jim and family moved to the cottage at 67 Harbour Terrace, which was next to his parents' house at No 65 Harbour Terrace. Over the years Jim used his skills to renovate the cottage and eventually he and Agnes moved into the house at No 65 where the family tradition of hospitality continued. Around 1960 a Golden Kiwi lottery win for Agnes and Jim made life easier in terms of property ownership.

Jim enjoyed his cars and we have a 1930s photo of him with his first car, outside the Harbour Terrace cottage. In later year years Jim and Agnes enjoyed travelling around and visiting family.

His grandchildren remember Jim as a loving and generous granddad who told them stories in bed. He was proud of his garden which had the excitement of hens at the back and which always produced new potatoes for Christmas dinner.

Above: **Jim and Agnes**

Lawrence Gerard McMullan (Larry)

Lawrence was born at home in Gabriels Gully in September 1911 and baptised at St Patricks, Lawrence. The McMullan family now had 4 children – 2 older sisters and 2 younger brothers. Early stories of Larry, some of them already told, join him with his older brother Jim and centre on pranks.

Like the other children, Larry attended the Lawrence St Patricks Church School in the 1872 building that still sits on its hillside. The school served Larry well as he gained a scholarship to Otago Boy's High School in Dunedin.

The scholarship was one driver for the family to move from Lawrence to Dunedin in the early 1920s. The family folklore recalls how the Parish Priest visited Larry's mother to tell her she was excommunicated from the Church because it was against Church Law to have a Catholic child at a non-Catholic school. She ignored him, and continued to practice her Faith!

Peter McIntyre, a noted New Zealand painter, was also at Otago Boy's High School and possibly in the same class. The way Larry told things it was if he had done the paintings for Peter McIntyre!

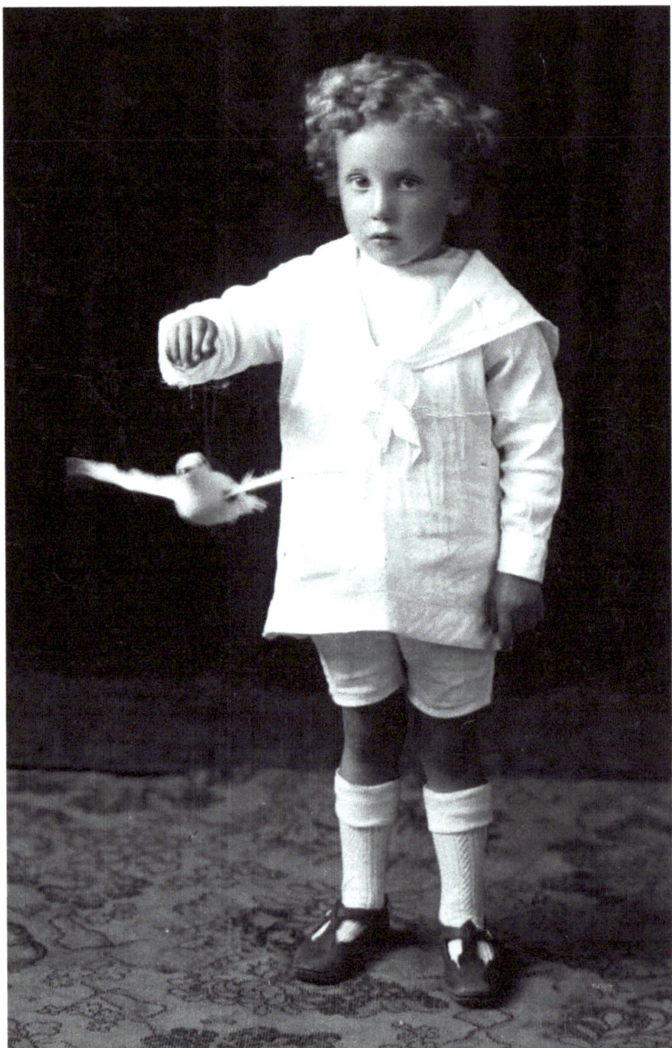

*Above: **An early photo of Larry** – presumably at a photographer's studio in Lawrence!*

After High School Larry got a Civil Service cadetship which meant a move north to Wellington where he probably boarded in the cadet hostel at the end of Oriental Bay. The photos by street photographers of the day show Larry as a well-dressed man about town. He also sent his mother a signed print of himself in full tennis gear. He made some return visits to Dunedin, once with his fiancé Agnes Randall.

Larry and Agnes met at the Northland Tennis Club and after a long engagement they were married in 1939 at 'The Basilica' on Hill Street, now the Sacred Heart Cathedral. Larry's mother Beatrice attended, his sister Dorothy was a bridesmaid, and Gabrielle Dunne remembers being a young flowergirl.

Larry was drafted into the army and sent to the New Zealand base in Egypt. The posting was deferred until after the birth of his son Randall in September 1944. So, without danger, he had an 'Overseas Experience' tour of Egypt, The Holy Land and Italy. He lived on those memories but the many retellings of them were sadly unappreciated by his family.

Sometime in the 1930s Larry changed the spelling of his name from 'Lawrence' to 'Laurence'. He never mentioned doing so but his birth certificate is definitely different to his death certificate - continuing a family tradition of 'tweaking' the spellings of names!

Left: **Larry McMullan and fiancé Agnes Randall** – at a 1930's ball in Wellington

Nickname: In his North Island life Larry was universally known to family and friends as *Mac*

In 1953 Larry and family moved from Island Bay, Wellington to Napier's very flat suburb of Marewa, created from the swamp just 22 years before in the big earthquake. Larry's job was now in the Ministry of Works as the District Land Purchase Officer for the East Coast region. In this capacity he travelled as far as East Cape amicably negotiating the government purchase of land from Iwi for roads and schools – it was easier times before Waitangi Treaty Settlements came into play.

Larry had an opportunity to return to Wellington to head up the Land Purchase division. But with children at high school his family were now happily embedded in Napier life, as was he. Upon retirement around 1971 Larry did at least one trip 'South' where he and brother Jim travelled around and remembered, if not recreated, some of their youthful pranks.

Like his brother Jim, Larry took refuge in his veggie garden and in the garden shed which sometimes contained brews not connected with gardening. Otherwise he was up at the Bluff Hill Bowling Club in his whites, and usually seen with his trademark of sucking on a pipe

Jessie Margaret McMullan

Jessie was born in Gabriels Gully in April 1914 and was baptised in the St Patrick's Church. She went to St Patrick's school Lawrence and then to St Dominic's College in Dunedin. In Dunedin she spent some time living with her Howe-Johns aunts – Annie, whose husband John O'Connor died when young, and Susie who was a home economics teacher. These aunts bought Jessie a new bicycle which made her the envy of her younger siblings. Young Jessie excelled at Highland Dancing, won many medals and, when she was 12, danced at the International Exhibition in 1926.

Above: **Jessie with young Gabrielle** – at Rooney's farm 1939

Jessie did her Nursing training in Oamaru. Gabrielle Dunne recalls how, when a young child, she had bubble baths in the Oamaru Nurses Home and received a lot of attention from Jessie and her nursing friends. Jessie was also Gabrielle's Godmother and took her caring duties seriously and Gabrielle remembers many holidays with the Hall family.

Above: Jessie as nurse at Milton

Jessie was a good seamstress and did lovely embroidery, a skill perhaps received from her mother. She was good baker and caterer and, living in Dunedin, she was there to help wider family members with celebrations for 21st birthdays, graduations, birthdays and pre-wedding parties.

Jessie enjoyed a day out shopping and a highlight of the event would be afternoon tea at the renowned Savoy Tearooms. In addition to being a homemaker, Jessie enjoyed being a relief nurse at times.

Annie Teresa McMullan (Nancy)

Annie, called Nancy, was born at home in September 1915 and was baptised at home a few days later by Father Kaverney. Perhaps it was illness that triggered the private baptism where the godparents are listed as Lawrence (aged 4) and Mary (Molly). However Nancy lived and went to St Patrick's school in Lawrence and then to Holy Name School in Dunedin.

She lived at home with her parents and was good at baking and decorating cakes. Nancy was also noted as being a great knitter and for enjoying all craft works. In later years she took up painting with water colours.

Nancy had a caring disposition and made gifts to give away – she made Christmas and birthdays special for many family members. She did housekeeping for her parents and then for the Casey family. Nancy also met John McCallion who worked in the mailroom of the Dunedin Post Office and was a relative of Jim's wife, Agnes.

Nancy and John married and lived in Corstorphine, Dunedin where they had four children. Alas, John died young in 1956 and Nancy raised four young children by herself. She needed all her skills in housekeeping and craftwork. Nancy is remembered as always being hospitable and for welcoming company.

Left: **Nancy and her father Tom**.

Dressed for a wedding – perhaps that of Nancy herself to John McCallion.

Kathleen Alannah McMullan

Kathleen was born at home in Gabriels Gully in April 1917 and baptized in St Patrick's Church Lawrence by Father John Lynch. Her main schooling was in Dunedin at Sacred Heart School, North East Valley where she remembered the planting of trees in front of Santa Sabina Convent – they were removed in 2013.

As a young woman Kathleen lived at home in Harbour Terrace, Dunedin and worked at the McKenzies department store in central Dunedin. Friday night was 'late night shopping' and Kathleen and Dorothy were known to bring material home after shopping on Friday for their mother to make dresses, to wear at a dance on the Saturday evening!

In 1939 Kathleen married Ron Cox and at first they lived with Ron's parents at Bayfield Road. They then lived in a State House at Johnson Sreet, Milton. The family later lived in Oamaru, then Mosgiel.

Kathleen was a homemaker extraordinaire, an amazing baker and was very hospitable. She loved company and there are many memories of Kathleen sitting with her feet inside the oven of her coal range. This was a regular occurrence!

Kathleen was a good basketball player, coach and referee. She biked round the village in Milton, loved movies, and she and Ron formed a strong pair in the game of darts. At every opportunity Kathleen visited her sister, Dorothy, at the orchard in Alexandra. She is remembered for having to put on her "lippy" before meeting Dorothy. They were great mates

Kathleen loved her nieces and nephews and was always supportive of them – even to placing $1 bets on Barry's racehorse, 'Archie's Pal'. As this horse was always in the money for a place, Kathleen's winnings joined her savings into a little black bag. This bag was 'hidden' in her bedroom and, as children, the nieces and nephews used to love counting her money.

Above: **Babe and Kathleen** – and fox furs

Kathleen had a period of writing her name as *Kathlyn*, which she considered looked more pretty. It also continued a family tradition of 'looseness' about name spellings.

Blossom Festivals in Alexandra were annual social highlights and on one occasion, Kathleen brought a bottle of gin to the orchard so that the girls could have a drink while the men went to the Clyde Pub. The bottle turned out to contain water, not gin, so Kathleen, Dorothy and Gabrielle were left to drink tonic water!

Left:
Bride Dorothy with her father Tom. Kaye Wilson on left and Kathleen on right.
Taken August 1942 on the steps of St Joseph's Cathedral, Dunedin

Dorothy Frances

Dorothy was last child of Beatrice and Tom and, like her older siblings, she was born in the cottage at Gabriels Gully and was baptised at St Patrick's Church, Lawrence. She went to Sacred Heart School, North East Valley, Dunedin followed by St Dominic's College.

As a teenager Dorothy loved movies and collected photos of film stars for her bedroom walls. Dorothy worked at McKenzies store for a period before starting nursing training at Napier Hospital. Meanwhile, with her sister Kathleen, Dorothy enjoyed the dances at the Town Hall and often wore an evening dress made by her mother, at short notice.

Dorothy spent her holidays on the Rooney farm in Oamaru. where she enjoyed a special bond with her older sister, Beatrice. When she was bridesmaid at the wedding of Larry and Agnes in Wellington, Gabrielle recalls Dorothy dancing in the street along with the bride and bridal party. She had a beautiful soprano voice and sang in the Dunedin Town Hall.

Dorothy always loved music, played the piano by ear and all her family learned the piano at her insistence. She once spent some Insurance money buying a piano

Dorothy married Alec Wilson as soon as he returned from World War II in 1942. She left her nurse training in Napier and met him off the boat in Wellington. They initially lived in a flat in Tabert St Alexandra, from where Alec biked out to plant the early orchard by day and worked on the gold dredge by night. Dorothy worked in the Milk Bar below the flat. In addition to managing her family at The Orchard on Dunstan Road Dorothy enjoyed playing golf and was an active member of the Catholic Women's League and the Church Choir.

When Dorothy heard anyone coming up the orchard drive she would hurry to the mirror to tidy hair and put on lipstick. Some family members continue this tradition - 'you must have your lippy on to feel good'!

Above: **Dorothy and Alex Wilson at front. Newell Wilson behind**. At the Rooney's Farm

Dorothy had an enthusiasm for fashion which she shared her sister Kathleen and other family members. She purchased clothes in Alexandra at Hewitt's Drapery store or the branch of Arthur Barnett's department store. Dorothy would hide new clothes under the bed and slowly introduce them. But reckoning could come when Alex, doing the accounts in the sunroom, would issue a roar: 'Dorothy, what is all this you bought at Arthur Barnett's!'

In retirement Dorothy and Alex lived in Ashworth Street Alexandra, enjoyed their children and grandchildren and did some overseas travel. They eventually moved to the Ranui rest home in Alexandra where both lived into the 20th Century.

Later Years of Beatrice and Tom

In Dunedin Tom worked in the Harbour Board office. Babe remembered that each week he handed over his complete wages to Beatrice who did the financial organising while Tom tended the garden.

Beatrice's grandchildren, such as Beatrice McDermott and Gabrielle Dunne, recall their Nana in her later life as being a gentle and gracious lady. She maintained her gift for sewing and could still look at a smart dress in a shop window, then go home and recreate it.

We have photos of Beatrice travelling to Wellington for Larry's wedding in 1939. She lived out her Catholic Faith and walked to the Cathedral to attend 6am Mass. Young Beatrice remembers walking to Mass with her Nana, along Anzac Avenue and up Stuart Street. They came home via the main streets to look in shop windows.

Alas, Beatrice died in 1941, at the early age of 66.

Above: **Beatrice McMullan** in later years

Tom lived on until 1958 so more grandchildren have memories of him. He often stayed at the Rooney farm in Oamaru travelling by train from Dunedin.

At dinner time on the evening of his arrival he gave Gabrielle, Margaret and Barry each a sixpenny coin. They were fascinated to play with the coins because they weren't accustomed to seeing money – everything was paid for by cheques. At the end of the meal they expected that Granddad would retrieve the coins – and he obliged every time!

Grandchildren Barry and Gabrielle Rooney remember keeping a healthy distance from Tom's walking stick – which he liked to hook around their ankles, or even their necks!

Each evening Granddad Tom would have two whiskies with milk. Father Kevin Kean, a curate in the Oamaru Parish, would time his visits well and both men became good friends. Granddad wanted to be buried by a Priest. He was baptised by Fr.Kean a few years before he died as apparently he had never been baptised but thought of himself as a Catholic. When the family was young, Tom dressed the children in their Sunday best for Beatrice to take them to Mass. In preparation, their shoes were polished on Saturday evenings

Above: **Tom in the 1890s** – as a young man about town

Left: **Tom in the 1950s** – as an older man about town

Even in retirement Tom always presented himself well in a 3-piece suit, complete with fob watch which he referred to often.

When Tom was unable to care for himself, the family arranged for him to go into the care of The Little Sisters of the Poor who were in Anderson's Bay in those days. His house was rented out to a family who stayed for a short time then shifted to Hyde, taking all the contents with them – even the carpets! His daughters Babe and Dorothy were the Trustees for the property and had worrying times before the goods were tracked down at Hyde, and returned.

At one stage it was arranged that Tom would spend three months at each of his daughters in turn but this didn't work well and he moved to the Milton Hospital for care of the elderly. He remained composed to the end although he would sometimes claim to muddle his children's names! And he never let on that he was actually two years older than his children believed and as his burial details record.

The Grandchildren of Thomas and Beatrice McMullan

Children of "Babe" McMullan and John ROONEY
Gabrielle Anne
Margaret Diane
John Barrymore "Barry"
Children of "Jim" MCMULLAN and Agnes McCallion
Beatrice Lorraine
Ann Susan
John Thomas
Children of "Larry" MCMULLAN and Agnes Randall
Randall
Lyndsay Margaret
Children of Jessie McMullan and Francis HALL
Diane Elizabeth
Barbara Frances
Children of "Nancy" McMullan and John MCCALLION
Ray
Annette
Peter
Stephen
Children of Kathleen McMullan and Ronald COX
Gaynor "Gaye"
Kenn
Jennifer
Allanah
Children of Dorothy McMullan and Alexander WILSON
Kathleen
Anne Marie
Michael
Jacqueline
John

Note: Most of these grandchildren of Tom and Beatrice now have children and grandchildren of their own!

Family Places

Left: McMullan Cottage Gabriels Gully

Family reunion March 2011

Otago Daily Times 22 Mar 2011:

Cottage owner Jeff Barlow and his wife Jenny bought the cottage in 1999 and were faced with a big restoration project. "The house had been let go - there were possums in the roof and walls, and it leaked." He said they had lived in the house for eight years without power or flushing toilets, and when they did get them it "took a while to get used to all the noises".

McMullan Cottage Gabriels Gully

After their marriage at Albertown in October 1899, the paper reports Thomas and Beatrice as leaving 'for their new home in Lawrence'. Tom already owned a modest Gabriels Gully property which started as a one-room rabbiter's hut.

Over the years Tom used his carpentry skills to build extensions and make a compact family home.

The cottage eventually consisted of two bedrooms, a lounge, a lean-to kitchen, beautiful panelled ceilings and an ornate front door. It is hard to believe the large family fitted into the space.

The cottage is on the east side of Gabriels Gully Road, at the entrance to the valley, about 100m from the road on a ledge of the rising hillside. It is just a short walk from the cottage to Lawrence where, as you cross a stream and the old railway route, you are looking up at hill where the buildings of St Patrick's Church and School sit.

A little further up the Gabriels Gully Road is the similar-sized cottage, called Cosy Dell, where the Howe-Johns grandparents lived with two of their daughters Annie and Susie.

The McMullan grandparents lived on the farm at Wetherstones, about 1 km out of Lawrence on the site of the present Golf Club.

All the children of Beatrice and Tom are recorded as being born at home in the cottage. They lived their childhood at The Cottage until they left Lawrence for boarding school or work. In the early 1920s the family moved to Dunedin for a variety of reasons but family links with Lawrence were ending in other ways as the children's grandparents peacefully died after long lives.

Above: Sketch of the cottage

The life of the cottage after the McMullan family is largely unknown until the early 1990s when a band of family members purchased and renovated the property as a holiday place. The labour and love that went into the project is outside the scope of this book and deserves a chronicle of its own. The family enjoyed the cottage again and had a reunion there. The property then passed to Jeff Barlow who, with his wife Jenny, valiantly continued the restoration. In 2011 the McMullan family had a reunion picnic lunch at the cottage as part of the Gabriels Gully 150th anniversary celebrations.

Lawrence town

In modern times Lawrence has survived as a town of about 500 inhabitants on the main road from Dunedin to Alexandra and Queenstown. Most of the notable town buildings the McMullan family knew still exist. To get an idea of how the town was regarded around the time of Tom and Beatrice the extracts nearby are from the 1905 *Cyclopedia of New Zealand*; a sort of Wikipedia of its day. The population at that time was about 1200 people.

Extract from 1905 *Cyclopedia of New Zealand*:

LAWRENCE , the chief town in the county of Tuapeka, is the terminus of the branch line from Milton, whence it is twenty-four miles distant. It is sixty miles by rail from Dunedin, with which it has communication twice daily, and there is a daily coach service between Lawrence and Roxburgh. There has been for many years a considerable, waggon traffic from Lawrence to the interior of Central Otago, but this is being gradually lessened in proportion with the progressive construction of the Otago Central Railway.

Lawrence, which, was named alter a celebrated English general, is the centre of a large mining and farming district. It came into existence with the gold "rush" to Gabriel's Gully, which is about two miles distant. This celebrated goldfield is a favourite place of interest with visitors, and in the surrounding district, gold mining is still carried on on an extensive scale by modern scientific methods. Sheep-farming is also carried oil, and stock sales are held fortnightly in the town. Lawrence is built for the most part on rising ground, and stands at an elevation of 356 feet above sea level,

Below: **View of Lawrence** in the early 1900s

Wetherstones area

The Wetherstones area is just a few kilometres from Lawrence and the old McMullan family of Thomas and Mary are listed in records as living at Wetherstones (Flat) from about 1870 until their deaths in 1918 and 1920. They possibly lived there from the time of their arrival from Ireland in the late 1860s. Their farmland, now the golf links, is on the 'flats' on the way from Lawrence to Wetherstones.

In the 1860's around 2000 miners worked in the hills around Wetherstones. The township had a post office, over a dozen hotels and a public school where McMullan children appear in the school records.

By 1900, gold digging had given way to farming with a few companies extracting gold by sluicing and dredging. And there were no hotels. Rather more durable was the *Hart's Black Horse Brewery* which didn't close until 1923. The brick arched foundations of the old brewery currently make a picturesque ruin amidst trees.

Extract from 1905 *Cyclopedia of New Zealand*:

The main streets of Lawrence are lighted with twenty-two kerosene lamps. The streets are wide, and the pavements are asphalted, while some of the roads in the residential parts of the town are edged with ornamental trees.

A cemetery, ten acres in extent, is prettily situated, on rising ground, on the Evan's Flat, road. The water supply is drawn from the head of the Gabriel's Gully creek, and brought along seven miles of open water race to the town reservoir.

Note: this is the water race that flowed in front of the McMullan Cottage

Below: **The Hart Family of 1910** in front of the Brewery at Wetherstones. Some young adults here probably attended the Wetherstones School with McMullan children

Family homes

The table below gives the locations of significant homes for Thomas and Beatrice McMullan. Also listed are the early family homes of their children.

Town	*Location*	*Notes*
Lawrence	Wetherstones farm Waipori Rd, No 27 approx Now Golf Club site	Family home of Tom's parents Thomas and Mary McMullin from 1870 to 1923 approx
Lawrence	Cosy Dell Cottage, Gabriels Gully Rd, No 79 approx	Later home of Beatrice's parents William and Mary Howe-Johns. Also home to Howe-Johns daughters Susie and Annie until 1920s
Lawrence	McMullan Cottage, Gabriels Gully Rd, No 18 approx	Family home of Tom and Beatrice McMullan from 1899 to 1923 approx
Dunedin	65 Harbour View Terrace, North Dunedin Now Hockey Centre site	McMullan family home from early 1920s until 1958 approx. Later home to Jim and Agnes McMullan and family
Dunedin	67 Harbour Terrace North Dunedin Now Hockey Centre site	Cottage next door to the house at 65. Home to Jim and Agnes McMullan and family
Oamaru	The Farm, Rooney's Road, Weston	Family home of Babe and John Rooney
Napier	30 Tom Parker Avenue, Marewa, Napier	Family home of Larry and Agnes McMullan from 1953 to 1977
Milton	51 Johnson St Miilton	Family home of Kathleen and Ron Cox
Dunedin	6 Milford Avenue, Carlton Hill, Dunedin	Family home of Nancy and John McCallion
Alexandra	Te Koanga Orchard Dunstan Road Alexandra	Family home of Dorothy and Alex Wilson

Family Schools and Churches

Above: Lawrence Catholic School, which also acted as the church before 1892. (Photo from Wiki Commons)

The religion followed by the families of Thomas McMullan and Beatrice Howe-Johns seems to have been set by the women; not uncommon in those times, or now.

Tom McMullan's mother, born as Mary Thomson, was married in the Church of Ireland (Anglican) church of St Tida, Bellarchy, Ireland. The McMullan/McMullin family she married is very likely to have been Presbyterian because of the Scottish links of the name. Mary is noted around 1916 as being 'staunch' Anglican and Mary and Thomas are buried together in the Anglican section of the Lawrence cemetery. Old Thomas was perhaps neutral in matters religious.

Beatrice's Howe-Johns' mother was born Mary Kelly and came from County Clare, Ireland and set the Catholic religion for their 7 or 8 children. William came from Devon and his father, Samuel Johns, is recorded as being baptised at the New Meeting House Presbytarian, Moreton Hampstead in 1803. Presumably William did not feel strongly about religion.

When young Thomas and Beatrice married at Albertown in 1899 it was Beatrice's faith that set the McMullan family as Catholic. But we can assume that it was not a divisive family matter as the McMullan family obviously interacted with their 'staunch-Anglican' grandmother McMullan round at the Wetherstones farm.

Wetherstones School

In the 1880s Thomas McMullan is recorded as attending the **Wetherstones Public School** and leaving it in 1887. He was 16 by birth but perhaps the wrong recording of his age had started. The school records record him leaving school to be a 'farm labourer'.

Later in his life, his grandchildren recall that he could still recite poems such as 'The boy stood on the burning deck' and 'Barbara Frietchie'. In the 1800s both these poems were common content in *School Readers,* the books used in schools to teach and encourage reading. Recitations were part of school lessons, and also popular at family and social occasions.

The boy stood on the burning deck
Whence all but he had fled;
The flame that lit the battle's wreck
Shone round him o'er the dead.

Yet beautiful and bright he stood,
As born to rule the storm;
A creature of heroic blood,
A proud, though childlike form.

Opening verses of the poem Casabianca by Felicia Hermans, Britain 1826.

Lawrence Catholic school

In Lawrence, **St Patrick's Church School** opened in 1872 as one of the first Catholic Schools established by Bishop Moran. The building served as both school and church until the new church was opened in 1892. A noted early head teacher at St Patrick's School was John Joseph Woods who in 1876 composed the music for *God Defend New Zealand* , that became the national anthem. Woods was also the choirmaster for St Patrick's church.

In 1893 the Dominican Sisters came to run St Patrick's school and the McMullan children were well-educated by those nuns. The St Patrick's school building still clings to the hill above the town and is a Category 1 Historic Place by virtue of its historical significance and architecture. The elegant design was by the prominent Dunedin architect Robert Lawson.

> God Defend New Zealand:
>
> *Being a choirmaster, Woods' focus in composing the melody was to make it simple and easy for children to sing. This proved to aid its success when the Premier George Grey visited Lawrence on 11 March 1878 and was welcomed by six hundred local schoolchildren singing what was by then beginning to be labelled as the "national anthem.*
>
> From Wikipedia

Other schools

Almost all the children attended St Patrick's school in Lawrence before moving to work or other schools listed below.

- Beatrice (Babe) – St Patrick's Dominican College *Teschemakers*, boarding school nr Oamaru
- Lawrence (Larry) – Otago Boys High School
- Jessie – St Dominic's College, Dunedin
- Nancy – Holy Name School, North Dunedin
- Kathleen – Sacred Heart School, North East Valley, Dunedin
- Dorothy – Sacred Heart School, North East Valley, Dunedin followed by St Dominic's College, Dunedin.

Lawrence Catholic church

Above: St Patrick's church Lawrence. The original brick was stuccoed in the 1920s

The St Patrick's church of Lawrence of 1892 replaced a corrugated iron church of 1864, which in turn had replaced the 1862 calico tent! The 1892 church still stands, and is another protected Historic Place. The exterior of the brick surfaces was roughcast in the 1920s, to protect the bricks and mortar. The interior of the church is unchanged in form except for continual enhancements by gifts, such as the stained glass windows.

All the McMullan children were baptised in this church, except Nancy who was baptised at home within days of birth because there were fears for her health. The children would have attended the church and heard the church choir directed by John Woods, the composer of *God Defend New Zealand.* We can excuse Dorothy, born in 1920, from remembering much as the family moved to Dunedin when she was 3 or 4.

The Catholic church in New Zealand of the late 1900s had become religiously divisive as the pragmatic colonial French legacy of Bishop Pompallier gave way to Irish clergy who encouraged a separate system of schools. Patrick Moran arrived in 1871 as the first Bishop of Dunedin along with 10 Dominican nuns as teachers.

In 1892, at the opening of the new St Patricks church in Lawrence, Bishop Moran gave a very strong, and long sermon on the topic of schools.

From the New Zealand Tablet, 15 January 1892 reporting Bishop Moran's words:

The State school system of education was destructive of the principles of religion; it blotted out the name of God from the human heart; and aimed at bringing men back to paganism again.

St Joseph's Cathedral, Dunedin

The Dunedin Cathedral, which opened in 1886, was another of Bishop Moran's building projects.

The Catholic newspaper *Tablet* paper on May 1895 lists donations being made to the Cathedral Building Fund and includes 'Mrs Howjohns' of Clyde giving 1 pound. All the donations were for £1, which was quite a sum of money for the time as the total building cost was £22,500 (approx. $45,000).

The 'Mrs Howjohns' would have been Mary, the mother of Beatrice McMullan's. Later, when living in Dunedin, Beatrice would walk to the Cathedral every morning for 6am Mass

Both Molly and Babe told a story that had taught them an important lesson. One Sunday, when at Mass in Sacred Heart Church in North East Valley Dunedin, their mother Beatrice put a half crown on the collection plate. Both girls knew that their mother couldn't afford to give that amount of money and were concerned.

After Mass, a man gave Mrs McMullan an envelope containing money to repay her husband for 'a long-owed debt'. The girls remembered this gem of wise thinking and action and passed it on to their siblings!

Beatrice and Tom would see four of their children married in the Cathedral:

- Jim in May 1928,
- Kathleen in 1939,
- Jessie in April 1940, and
- Dorothy in August 1942.

The McMullan christening gown

The Christening gown that all the McMullan siblings wore at their Baptisms is back home in Lawrence – now under the watchful eye of the Tuapeka Museum.

For thirty five years it was in the good care of Chriss Spooner, Jim McMullan's granddaughter. With help from her mother, Mary, and expertise care of a friend at Auckland Museum, (a fabric and painting restoration artist) they were able to remove rust marks, clean and mend the little holes. Fortunately it was wrapped in acid-free protective paper.

The Christening gown has the following features.

- The little white gown approx. is approx. 80 cms in length.
- The material is fine polished linen with a slight sheen, and small pleats join the bodice to the skirt at the waist.
- Six rows of pintucks and hand embroidered eyelet lace are around the lower skirt.
- Beautifully embroidered lace is in the centre front of bodice and the back ties with little tapes.
- The sleeves are short, embroidered lace at the lower edges. and at one time would've been puffy.

Left: **The McMullan christening gown worn by one of the children** – possibly Jim at the time of the photo on page 13

Considering the age of the McMullan Christening gown (over 110 years), it is in remarkable condition. The family is grateful to Chriss Spooner for looking after the gown and giving it to the Lawrence Museum for safe-keeping and for future families to view.

Below: **Family group at Dunedin House, late 1930s**
Jim McMullan, Agnes McMullan (Jim's wife), Agnes Randall (soon to be Larry's wife), Beatrice and Tom. With young Beatrice McDermott in front

From Photo Albums

Above: **Dorothy**

Below: **Jessie**

Above: **Nancy** with husband John and baby Ray

Below: **Beatrice with John Rooney, and young Gabrielle** – Nelson 1939

Above: **Babe** with John Rooney

Left: **Jim** in front of Harbour Tce cottage

Below: ***Larry and Jim*** return to Gabriels Gully in the 1970s

The McMullan Cottage, Gabriels Gully, 2011

Above: The kitchen range

Below: Grandchildren and Great grandchildren of Tom and Beatrice McMullan, and friends. March 2011

Above: Detail of cottage woodwork
Rescued by family members but then lovingly restored by the current owner of the cottage Jeff Barlow, whom the family thanks for his work and hospitality.

Early Family Landscapes and Seascapes

Above: **View of Bickington Village** with Dartmoor in background

Bickington, Devon

Birthplace of William Howe-Johns

Bickington and its neighbourhood occupies a strip of South Devon between the high ground of Dartmoor and the sea at Teignmouth. The area is within 10 kilometres of Newton Abbot where the 1846 railway rapidly grew the town and within 10 kilometres of Ashburton which was an old centre of tin-mining.

Today the nearby A38 Devon Expressway speeds traffic further down the peninsular to Plymouth and Cornwall. But most of the local roads are the popular vision of quiet, lush and narrow English country lanes with the tall hedges trying to meet overhead.

A few kilometres to the West the land rises to Dartmoor where trees run out and the barren landscape features rocky outcrops called *tors* and the remains of stone age settlements. William Johns would meet a similarly stark landscape in Central Otago.

Neolithic people started to farm on Darmoor from around 3500 BC and leave the granite remains of England's earliest buildings. Early settlement on the slopes near Bickington was probably connected with the extraction of tin which was needed to make bronze weapons and articles.

Bickington is still a 'scattered' village with houses spread along the lanes, such as *Love Lane* and *Old Hill* that lead from the Lemon stream up to the church of St Mary at a junction. Around the church the oldest granite houses huddle low with many extensions added on over the centuries.

> BICKINGTON, a scattered village on the banks of the Lemon rivulet, and on the Exeter road, 3 miles N.E. of Ashburton, has in its parish 1375 acres and 374 inhabitants. The manor was dismembered many years ago, and the soil belongs to various freeholders. Here is a serge manufactory, employing 150 hands.
>
> *From White's Devonshire Directory 1850*

Above: **Map of South Devon**

Past residents of the Bickington area would recognise the same cottages, narrow lanes and lush hedges of the area today. But the cottages are now very comfortable and desirable. Cars need to negotiate how to pass on the narrow lanes and the tall hedges usefully hide some signs of modern life, such as parks of holiday caravans.

Church of St Mary the Virgin Bickington

Listed Grade I English Heritage Building:

Parish church. C15 with early C16 north aisle, late C19 south porch and vestry,
and late C19 or early C20 boiler house. C14 window, probably re-used, in tower.
Church was thoroughly restored in 1883-4; south wall, south porch, and east and
west gables of north aisle rebuilt.

Source: English Heritage

Above: **St Marys Church,** Bickington. Showing Lynchgate to cemetery with room above gate.

Below: **Love Lane Cottages**, Bickington. Census address of the Johns family for some decades, but not necessarily the same buildings.

Up until the 1800s most people lived and married in or within walking distance of their original town or village. Records show members of the wider Johns family living in or near the following places in that part of Devon: Ashburton, Bickington, Bovey Tracey, Ilsington, Manaton. Moretonhampstead and Newton Abbot.

By the 1850s farming and cloth-making in Devon was declining and this coincided with easier travel, such as on the new railways, and common knowledge of immigration to new countries.

In the 1851 census the 13 year old William Johns is recorded as being an agricultural labourer living on the Mann family farm at Gale near Bickington. We next hear of him as a New Zealand miner when he married Mary Kelly in Dunedin.

Left: **Gale Cottages** near Bickington. Possibly the workplace and home of William Johns in 1851. The windows and doors at the end of the building are modern.

Spooky Dartmoor

The special atmosphere of Dartmoor features in Conan Doyle's Sherlock Holmes story *The Hound of the Baskervilles*

Migrant Ships

The Warrior Queen

The McMullin-Thompson family travelled to New Zealand from the north of Ireland in 1867 or 1868. The connecting ferry and rail links from Belfast to London were well-established and the family sailed from London Docks to Port Chalmers (Dunedin). Their ship, the *Warrior Queen* of the Shaw Savill Company, was not fitted as a crowded migrant ship but is described as having comfortable accommodation for about seventy saloon and second class passengers. About fifty passengers on average were carried on its nine voyages to New Zealand between 1865 and 1874. A typical non-stop sailing lasted 90 days.

The Passengers
Thomas McMullin, Mary McMullin and infant son *Hugh McMullin. They were accompanied by Mary's mother Ann, brother Jim Thompson and her sister Margaret.*

The ship did carry assisted immigrants sponsored by the Provincial Government of Otago and the McMullin family may have been among these.

The Warrior Queen was a three-masted sailing ship built of oak in Sunderland, England, in 1856. It was described as frigate-built because of its single deck, similar to a navy frigate of the age. 'Blackwall Frigates' had a highly-rounded hull at the bow and were relatively fast sailing ships, although not as fast as the slightly later 'clipper' ships. At 988 tons she was of average size for the time.

Migrant sailing ships leaving London Docks were first towed by steam tug down the Thames to Gravesend in Kent. Another tug and pilot then took them through the Thames estuary around to the Downs near Deal where they waited for favourable winds.

The sailing ships had also refined the skill of sailing non-stop between England and New Zealand or Australia by taking a course that made use of prevailing winds and followed an approximation of the shortest 'Great Circle' route.

On this route ships no longer called at the agreeable port of Cape Town, as Captain Cook did several times. Instead they headed south into the Antarctica Ocean and followed a curving easterly route reaching around 50 degree of latitude which was south of land masses.

On some trips the Warrior Queen reported sighting some of the few islands in the Southern Ocean such as The Crozets and Possession Island.

Above: **The Warrior Queen**

Below: **Typical Advertisement**
From *Barrow's Worcester Journal*, September 1867

EMIGRATION TO
OTAGO, NEW ZEALAND.
ALTERATION OF TERMS.
ASSISTED PASSAGES GRANTED TO AGRICULTURAL LABOURERS, SHEPHERDS AND THEIR FAMILIES, AND FEMALE DOMESTIC SERVANTS.
SHIP "WARRIOR QUEEN," FIXED FOR END OF OCTOBER.

IN consequence of the great and increasing demand for AGRICULTURAL LABOUR, and the present high rate of Wages in this Province, the Home Agent has been authorized to continue the assistance formerly given to SINGLE FEMALE DOMESTIC SERVANTS, and to assist also approved AGRICULTURAL LABOURERS, SHEPHERDS and their Families.

The favourite first-class Passenger Ship "WARRIOR QUEEN," 13 years A 1 at Lloyds, 988 Tons Register, one of Messrs. Shaw, Savill, and Co.'s well-known Line of Packets, will Sail from LONDON for OTAGO direct towards the end of OCTOBER.

A duly qualified Surgeon will accompany the Ship.

Parties eligible to receive assistance, and others intending to pay their own Passage Money, will receive full information on applying to

GEORGE ANDREW, Secretary,
Otago Office,
60, Princess Street, Edinburgh, or to
B. G. DAY, ESQ., Quay Street, Worcester.

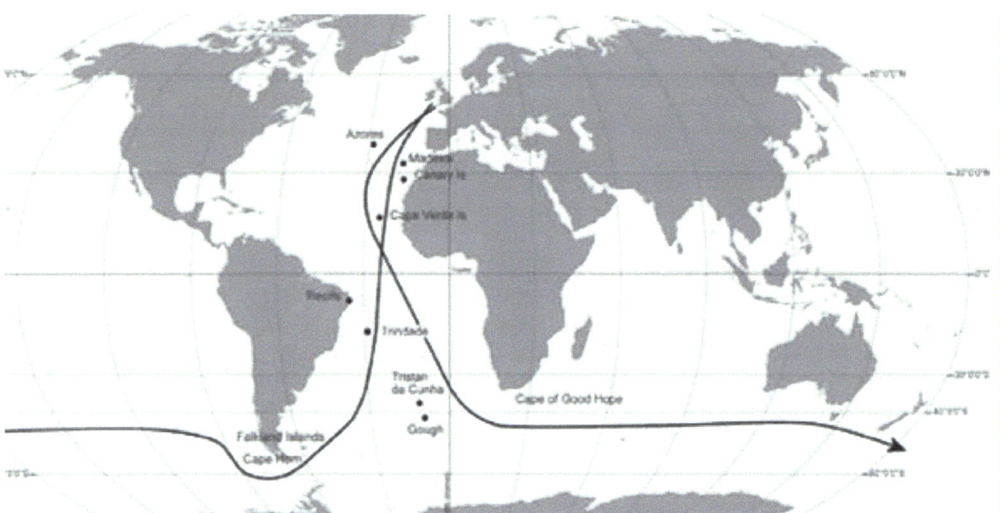

Above: **Typical sailing route –** southwards then eastwards with the winds

By the 1860s passenger steamships were common across the Atlantic between Europe and North America. But steamships consumed a lot of coal and were not economical on the run to New Zealand and Australia until the 1880s, by which time the Suez Canal had also opened a shorter route. By travelling in sailing ships driven by wind power our ancestors were 'Green' before their time!

Report of a Voyage

Extracts from the *Otago Witness* newspaper, 13 March 1869

Arrival of the ship Warrior Queen.
The frigate built ship Warrior Queen, arrived at the Heads from London on Monday, and was towed up to a discharging and loading berth by the steamtug *Geelong* at noon on Tuesday. Her passengers and luggage were brought to Dunedin by the local steamer *Golden Age* on her afternoon trip. The Warrior Queen has made a longer passage than usual, which is owing principally to three weeks' detention in the Bay of Biscay by heavy S.W. and westerly winds.

The Eqator was crossed on the 4th January in long. 20.30 W. The SE. trades continued until she reached lat. 25.27 S. when the wind hauled round to the northward and westward. The meridian of Greenwich was crossed on the 27th of January, and that, of the Cape on the 31st. Her easting for the most part was run down between the parallels of lat. 48 and 49 S. , and was characterised by extaordinarily heavy weather, during which she carried away her maintopsail yard and portquarter gallery, filling the cabin with water.

On the 18th and 19th of February she ran through between the Crozets, and sighted Possession Island. In long. 106 E on the 20th of February, she sighted a large iceberg, and passed other bergs on the two following days. ... The Snares were sighted at 1 a.m. on the 6th, and Stewart's Island at 5 the same evening

The Warrior is still in command of Captain A. Wilson, with whom is his old chief officer, Mr Taylor, and several of his former crew. She brings about 1500 tons of cargo, aud 57passengers, the latter having enjoyed good health throughout the trip, no sickness having occurred of an infectious nature. On arrival, the passengers expressed themselves as well satisfied with the ship and the treatment of her commander and officers.

Above: **At sea in a sailing ship**

End of the Warrior Queen

In September 1874 the *Otago Witness* reported from Northern California how the end of the *Warrior Queen*

The Warrior Queen was spoken at 5 o'clock p.m. on the 19th instant and at 6.30 p.m, without any idea that the ship was in any danger, she struck heavily, and although the wind was light, in fact almost calm, she went well up on the rocks, about five miles north of Point Reyes. ... The ship's boats, three in number, were launched, and the crew, numbering some twenty-seven, all told, were put in them. The captain remained aboard the ship all night, which was not a very desirable position for one not knowing on what part of the coast he was. At four o'clock in the morning he arrived at the conclusion that nothing could be done to save the ship ; he reluctantly set about saving the chronometers and personal effects of himself and crew, which they succeeded in doing to a certain extent, and the ship was abandoned, at which time she was lying easy, with 3½ feet of water in the hold.

The reports of the Warrior Queen's many calls at Dunedin, together with the above report, may have helped the family remember the ship's name.

The Rhea Sylvia

Mary Kelly came to Canterbury, New Zealand in 1861 in the ship *Rhea Sylvia*. She appears in the shipping lists as a single woman 'farm servant' immigrant from Galway, sponsored by the Provincial Government of Canterbury. Mary was to marry William Johns in Dunedin in 1863 and among their children was Beatrice Howe-Johns who married Thomas McMullan in 1899.

Report of the Voyage

Extracts from the *Lyttleton Times*, 8 May 1861

THE RHEA SYLVIA - This fine ship, which arrived on Monday, May 6th, 'left King's road, Bristol, on the 15th January, with 115½ adult emigrants, viz with the addition of an infant born on the voyage, she has brought to their destination, safely and without a single accident. There are in addition seven saloon and five 2nd cabin passengers. Among the emigrants is included a fair sprinkling of all crafts and callings: the men appear stout and ablebodied fellow, and the conduct of the unmarried women has been creditable.

The Rhea Sylvia is an easy, comfortable ship of 882 tons, with airy commodious 'tween decks. That she has not made a rapid passage is to be attributed solely to most preversel winds and unpropitious weather hardly had she cleared theEnglbh coast, when she was met by a succession of gales from S.S.W. and S.W., which raged from that quarter without any shift for a fortnight, and with such violence as to cause apprehension oocasionally to the most experienced.

It would be unfair to conclude this notice without stating that the kindness and attention of the commander, Mr.C.Evans, and his tact and judgment in the peculiar circumstances, often of a nature not altogether pleasant, which must arise in the control of a large and motley assemblage, are highly spoken of and gratefully acknowledged by the body of passengers.

Below: At Port Chalmers Dunedin Similar ships to the **Warrior Queen** and the **Rhea Sylvia**

The Voyage
Rhea Sylvia
A1 Clipper Ship 881 Tons, Departed Bristol 14 Jan 1861, Arrived Lyttleton 2 May 1861.

Ship named after the mythical mother of Romulus and Remus, founders of Rome

CHRISTCHURCH
CIRCULATING LIBRARY.

AN ADDITIONAL case of popular novelties now landing, ex Rhea Sylvia, also,
Account books, all rulings, well bound
German tree ornaments
Writing cases, desks, and boxes
German cabas and leather bags
Church services, prayers and bibles
Pocket and memorandum books
Winsor and Newton's color boxes
Boys' ditto, all sizes and prices
Novels, newest, best, and cheapest
Toys, work boxes, slates, games
Magic lanterns, all prices
Purses, French, German, and English
&c., &c., &c.

FROM BRISTOL FOR CANTERBURY, NEW ZEALAND.

TO SAIL on 12th JANUARY, 1861, conveying Passengers assisted under the auspicies of the Provincial Government of Canterbury, the splendid A 1 Clipper ship
"*RHEA SYLVIA*,"
881 Tons Register, 1,800 Tons Burthen.
CHARLES EVANS, Commander.

This Ship has beaten some of the fastest Ships out of any Port. On her last voyage from Bristol to Melbourne she anticipated the Overland Mails by several days. Her Saloon is arranged with Ladies' Boudoir, Bath-room, &c., and all her accommodation is superior to any Ships loading from any Port for New Zealand.

For particulars of Freight or Passage, apply to MILES BROTHERS and CO., 61, Queen-sq., Bristol.

Sailors
It was common for seaman to desert their ships, particularly at the places of gold rushes in California, Australia, and Otago. In Dunedin, constables were paid a reward for returning a seaman to his ship as that saved the captain having to hire a local man at a more expensive rate.
Family stories say that *William (Howe) Johns* 'jumped ship' to go the Otago gold rush at Gabriels Gully which started in 1861. Mary Kelly, who arrived in Christchurch in 1861, married William Johns in Dunedin in March 1863. We don't know how they met.

Further Information 2018

Castledawson, Co Derry/Londonderry

Hugh Thompson was born in 1811 and died, aged 53, in 1864. His wife was Ann Malone sometimes called Nancy. They lived on the eastern edges of the village of Castledawson in County Derry/Londonderry, Ireland. The location of his death and of his children's births is recorded as being in the Townsland of 'Leitrim'; there is still a Leitrim Rd on the edge of Castledawson.

Castledawson is within a few kilometres of other townships, such as Bellaghy and Maghera, mentioned in family documents.

Names
County Londonderry was used in documents of the time but *County Derry* is preferred by the Catholic community.
Castle Dawson was an alternative spelling for the town.

Hugh Thompson is listed in the Griffith's Valuation records of 1859 as renting and farming 2 plots of land near Hillhead Road. The plots comprised 'house, offices and land' and one of them is shared with James Thompson, probably Hugh's son. Modern satellite views of this land, on the next page, still show the same field pattern and an isolated building in one corner of the plot.

The Cookstown branch of the Belfast and Ballymena railway line which opened in 1856 had cut the plot of land into two areas. The existence of the railway, with connections from Castledawson station to Belfast, and onwards to Liverpool and London, would have made the processes of migration relatively easy to think about.

		Land, . . .	2	3	20
		Brick-field, . .		—	
James Thompson, Hugh Thompson,	Robert P. Dawson,	House, offices, & land, House, offices, & land,	8	0	0
Hugh Bates, . .	Same, . .	Land, . . .	2	2	5

Above: Extract from valuation records

In February 1864, Hugh Thompson died at home in Castledawson, aged 53. The cause of death is listed as as an 'abdominal tumour 12 weeks certified'. This event probably prompted the remaining family members to leave Castledawson for Otago New Zealand where Elizabeth Thompson (now Pearson) had been established in Wetherstons, Lawrence since 1862. She was joined by her sister Sarah Thompson (now Anderson) around 1864. We can speculate that they wrote home to Castledawson and the remaining Thompson family therefore had a target destination for their migration from Ireland.

Australian Connections

Members of the Thompson and McMullin families migrated directly to New Zealand in 1866. But some years earlier, two of the Thompson sisters had travelled, probably separately, to the goldfields of Victoria. They both married there and eventually moved on to the Otago goldfields in New Zealand, at Wetherstons near Lawrence.

Elizabeth Thompson emigrated to Victoria in the late 1850s and, in 1860, she married **John Pearson** and had a son. In 1861. John Pearson went to the gold diggings at Gabriels Gully, Otago and, after 4 months, returned to Victoria and brought his wife and son to Wetherstons.

In 1859 **Samuel Anderson** from the Maghera area of county Derry/Londonderry emigrated to the goldfields of Victoria with, according to his 1904 obituary, a 'number of schoolmates'. They travelled in the steam clipper ship, Royal Charter, which on its return voyage is noted for having been wrecked on the coast of Anglesey, Wales with great loss of life, and gold.

Sarah Thompson also emigrated to Victoria, possibly arriving in 1860 on the ship Merlin. It seems probable that Sarah and Samuel knew one another from Ireland as their homes were just a few kilometres away from one another. In 1863 they shared the same address in Eaglehawk, Bendigo and were married at the Presbyterian Manse on 26 March 1863. Later shipping lists show possible entries for Sarah and Samuel sailing from Victoria to Otago, to go the goldfields at Wetherstons.

Eaglehawk was a gold-mining town in Victoria, Australia and is now a suburb within the City of Greater Bendigo

The McMullin-Thompson family sailed from London direct for Port Chalmers Dunedin on the *Warrior Queen*, probably on 6th October 1866. On board were Thomas McMullin, wife Mary (Thompson) with infant son Hugh, and Mary's newly-widowed mother Ann Thompson. Mary's siblings James and Margaret were probably also on board. We are fairly sure about the ship but have not yet found passenger lists.

Maps old and new of Thompson Property Castledawson

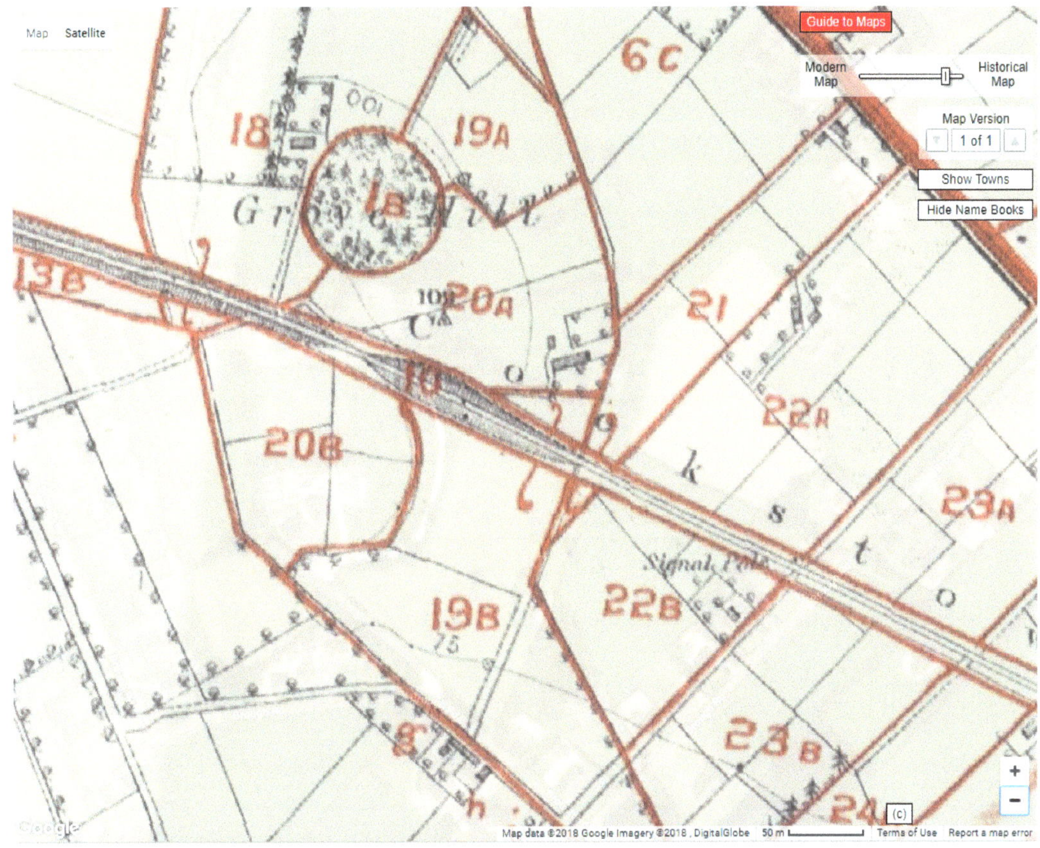

Left

1859 Valuation Map with Plot 20 divided by the 1856 railway into Plots 20a and 20b.

The building in the bottom right of plot 20a is probably the isolated one shown below

Left

Current map.

A building in the bottom right of plot 20a still exists but is isolated. Access would have been off Hillhead Road as Brough Rd was other side of railway

The ghost of the railway track remains.

The shape of the circular tree stand remains.

Wetherstones / Wetherstons, Otago, NZ

Left

'A Typical Miner's Residence 1870'

Left

'Westerstones of the present day 1911'

Photos from Master of Arts Thesis - *The history of Lawrence, Otago, New Zealand, from earliest times to 1921, including a review of its future prospects,* by M A Jennings, University of NZ (Canterbury), 1921

www.ingramcontent.com/pod-product-compliance
Ingram Content Group UK Ltd.
Pitfield, Milton Keynes, MK11 3LW, UK
UKHW060121300726
14090UKWH00002B/296

* 9 7 8 0 4 7 3 4 6 3 0 9 0 *